GREENLIGHT TO FREEDOM

A NORTH KOREAN DAUGHTER'S SEARCH FOR
HER MOTHER AND HERSELF

SONGMI HAN

CASEY LARTIGUE JR.

D1738841

*To Mom. For giving me life on this Earth,
a second life in South Korea,
and for being the Greenlight of my life.*

FSI PUBLISHING

66-5 Dongmak-ro
Mapo-gu, Seoul, South Korea.
First published in English in 2022 in the United States of America by
FSI Publishing.
Copyright © 2022 by FSI Publishing

www.fsi21.org

CONTENTS

FOREWORD

As a North Korean who was born into the core class of North Korea, I was lucky enough to be educated as an intellectual elite from a young age. I attended the best schools in the country and experienced a life that most other North Koreans could only dream of having. And as I joined the Foreign Ministry of North Korea, I was able to stay outside of North Korea, representing it abroad. My patriotism and loyalty seeped into my mind and body, blinding me from the reality of my own country.

But mindless patriotism only can last so long. As I faced countless discrepancies between cruel reality and the North Korea painted by the regime, my eyes slowly opened to the truth. My life has changed in many ways since I escaped to South Korea in 2016. I have learned more about my native country here than when I lived there and represented it abroad. My worst doubts about the welfare of my fellow countrymen came true as I look from the outside-in, with freedom of speech and thought. I acquired a better understanding of how most North Koreans live.

Greenlight to Freedom, written by Songmi Han with Casey Lartigue, is an eye-opener not only for people like me but also for those who know little about North Korea. Ms. Han grew up in the countryside of North Korea. She attended elementary school for only one year and barely survived by eating grass. The book follows her life from famine to freedom.

As many others do, it seemed natural that North Koreans would thrive once gaining freedom. But Ms. Han's story, along with those of other North Korean refugees, makes it clear that freedom isn't enough. There are still lingering issues and trauma that many must overcome before they can live satisfactory lives. With raw honesty, Ms. Han opens up about her life and shares the challenges she faced growing up and escaping from North Korea.

As I read her story, I thought about where I was at those times in my life, living a privileged life in North Korea and abroad. At that same time, there had been North Koreans like Ms. Han who were barely surviving. Many, regrettably, end up dying in the streets and at train stations from starvation and frostbite.

While all of this has been going on, the leadership builds nuclear weapons and engages in dangerous brinksmanship with global powers. North Korea's anti-human rights system is unprecedented in history. It is important that North Koreans who were not part of the elite tell their stories so that the world can see the side of North Korea that the regime tries to hide.

I hope that readers will be inspired to act on behalf of the North Koreans still stuck in the country as well as North Korean refugees who, like Ms. Han, have made it to freedom.

Tae Yong-ho
 A Member of the National Assembly of the Republic of Korea and a fellow survivor of the North Korean cruelty
 May 2022

INTRODUCTION

Over the past two decades, I have worked with many people with inspiring stories of overcoming challenges, ranging from low-income mothers seeking better education choices for their children in Washington, D.C., to North Korean refugees in South Korea bravely sharing their stories with the world despite threats from a dictatorship. The most unlikely author is Ms. Songmi Han.

When I first met Songmi in late 2019, she was struggling. She had found me after learning about Freedom Speakers International (FSI), which I co-founded with South Korean researcher Eunkoo Lee. Songmi wanted to improve her English as she was trying to take charge of her life. She was not the least bit interested in telling her story and had reasons to keep her identity concealed.

Before I knew it, she had already adopted me as her "life mentor." I hired her as a Special Assistant at FSI. She said that she was at last settled down. At the time, I was writing on a book about my decade of working with North Korean refugees. I mentioned in passing to Songmi that, based on the things she was telling me, she might want to write a book one day.

At first, she said no, but later, she considered it seriously, talked it over with her mom because they would be revealing some embarrassing things publicly, then finally drafted me to help her write it. I shelved my own manuscript and began working on hers. Writing her story seemed to be a form of therapy for her to heal her heart and to encourage others struggling with trauma, separation, and various mental health challenges.

There were numerous challenges in writing *Greenlight to Freedom*. For one, the book is written in English, which is Songmi's second language. Telling her story in English seemed to be both liberating and challenging for her. We worked without an interpreter or translator. At times, it became an English class as she learned Western idioms and English vocabulary and then began to internalize them. We hope that readers will understand that what we lose in flowery language is instead a presentation of Songmi's raw account of her experiences, emotions, and stories from her journey.

Second, as we worked on the book, she relived some trauma. We had to take more than one break during the interview and writing process. It became more comfortable for her to speak in the third person rather than first person. Speaking in the third person made her storytelling less painful and more objective. She also began to assert herself as she got more comfortable with telling her story. She gained new perspectives on some of the people in her life, including some that she had tried to forget. This meant revising parts of the book along the way and after the alleged final version was done.

Third, North Korea is not a normal country.

Numerous North Korean refugees have expressed concern about opening their lives to readers and listeners who can't understand the reality of North Korea. North Koreans grow up under the boot of a cult. The messengers have often found themselves and their loved ones judged. "How could you leave your family behind?" "How could you eat (fill-in-the-blank)?" "How could you (or your family) have acted that way?" My all-time favorite case of projecting one's own life onto North Koreans was the South Korean high school student who was completely serious when he asked at an event I moderated, "If North Koreans are starving, why don't they just order from Pizza Hut?" He was concerned, serious, and baffled, apparently, why things weren't as easy for North Koreans as they were for him living in the world 10th largest economic power.

Songmi shares many potentially embarrassing details about her family that could be fodder for insta-judgmental people. How, as co-author, could I tell Songmi's story in a way that people with knee-jerk responses could read it with their knees solidly in place? I hope that readers will read the entire book and not have snap judgments about individuals doing their best to survive North Korea. It may take reading the book a second time to understand some of the things that happened. Songmi survived North Korea and has come through it thankful. Hopefully, readers will share in her thankfulness and reserve their judgment for the North Korean regime that puts North Koreans in desperate no-win situations.

As I worked with Songmi, I was reminded of the 1845 *Narrative of the Life of Frederick Douglass* in which the former slave-turned abolitionist told much of his story up to that point. In the introduction, ardent abolitionist Wendell Phillips mentioned the Aesop fable "The Man and the Lion," where the lion complained that he would not be misrepresented "when the lions write history." Up to that point, slavery was usually presented from the perspective of slaveholders.

Similarly, much of the discussion about North Korea is focused on the North Korean regime, with reporters rushing to report on the latest oddball story out of North Korea. Although about 34,000 North Korean refugees have escaped from North to South Korea since the late 1990s, only a handful of books (about 20) have been published by North Korean refugees. As someone who has worked directly with almost 500 North Korean refugees over the last decade, I know that there are many incredible stories yet to be told.

One of them is by Songmi Han.

Unlike Mr. Douglass, Songmi is not an activist. Readers won't see discussions about the dictators of North Korea. She has not written a treatise explaining North Korea to researchers and reporters. This is a human-interest story by and about a young woman who happened to have been born in North Korea. From a historical perspective, it is of great importance that such accounts are preserved. And, more importantly, from a human perspective, there is much we can each learn as individuals through Songmi's journey, her perspective, and what she has overcome.

Casey Lartigue Jr.
   Co-Founder, Freedom Speakers International
   February 2022

PREFACE

Growing up in North Korea, I was a tomboy who wanted to play, run and wrestle. I was so active, I had so much energy, and I was constantly in motion as a child.

This turned out to be a disaster for my uncle who was often my babysitter. Uncle Gicheol had recently been discharged from the military after being diagnosed with tuberculosis. The 1990s were a tough time in North Korea; many people were dying of starvation and various diseases. Because he was too sick to work, he would be at home during the day, mainly reading, and keeping me from destroying the house.

I was three years old. I couldn't understand why he was so interested in reading all day. To distract him, I would throw a pillow at him. War had been declared in our living room. He would throw the pillow back at me, to let me know that he had accepted my challenge.

He was kind, like my grandma. He always talked so nicely, and he never got angry at me, although there were times that he should have. His voice was weak, his body was even weaker, frail. He was sick so often, but I wanted to play! Sometimes I would spill something, then my uncle would admonish me by having me stand in the corner.

When I did something wrong, or when he *thought* I had done something wrong, he would tell me: "Songmi-ya. Go. Stand in the corner on one foot." He would have me hold two arms up in the air as I stood on either my right or left foot, as instructed. When I got tired, I would secretly shift from one foot to the other. Without looking up, he would tell me in a stern voice: "I see you. Stand on your right foot only."

I was always amazed. He would be reading while directing me, without looking at me. "Stand up." "Down." "Up." "Down." Was he watching me or just reading those words "Up" and "Down" on the page? It seemed that he had an eye hidden on top of his head to watch me even as he was focused on a book.

"Uncle, I'm so tired. It hurts. I'm sorry. I won't do it again." My thighs and knees hurt so much going up and down.

"I can't hear you," he would say.

In a louder voice: "I won't do it again."

"Really? Can I believe you?"

I would promise him that I wouldn't do whatever I had just done, even if I had been caught for the second, third or whatever number of times. Eventually, probably after he had finished another chapter in a book, he would set me free from the corner. Then a few minutes later, another pillow would go flying past his head or into the back of his head if I had good aim.

After our battles during the day, my uncle would get serious. "Songmi-ya, now it is time to clean up." Others were out working, so we would quickly clean up before they got back. Then we would be happily cleaning together, my various crimes and his punishment long forgotten. I was happy during that time. I could smile and laugh so much with my family. I was laughing so much, even when others didn't see the humor. One time, my grandma asked, "Why are you laughing so much?"

"I don't know, everything is funny." Others would be laughing at me laughing at things.

However, once it was almost dinner time, everything would change. It would be difficult for me to laugh or play. For various reasons, as a child and as an adult, I have had to remind myself to smile, to love life like that three-year-old girl inside me once did. The following is about my struggle to smile, how I lost my voice for so long, why I am grateful for the good things that have happened to me, and how I was able to live life again with the Greenlight of my life.

Songmi Han
  February 2022

PART I

NORTH KOREA

SCARY FATHER

"*Are you ready?*"

There was no anger or emotion in my father's voice. It was neither a request nor a demand. The inevitable would occur every night, around 8 p.m., like a clock ticking second-by-second to an encounter that could not be avoided. Almost every night the following happened at our home, about 240 kilometers (150 miles) from North Korea's capital of Pyongyang.

My father, Mom, grandma and uncle would have dinner together, typically rice, stew, and some side dishes. The oldest (grandmother) and youngest (me) would talk the most before and during dinner as we gathered around the kitchen table. Grandma Bae and I were inseparable. My father, Mom and uncle were almost always quiet around dinner time.

After dinner, there was the usual clanging sounds as Mom washed the dishes. Another nice dinner done, I would dash to the living room, eager to entertain my grandma with the rhythmic gymnastics or something else I had learned at preschool. Nearby, but also far away, my father would be puffing on a cigarette farmed by Grandma Bae and that he had rolled himself. Uncle Gicheol usually would have slipped outside. As the clanging sounds from the kitchen started to subside, I could feel my face turning red, with tears forming in my eyes. Mom had taught me how to tell the time, but I dreaded knowing when it would be 8 p.m.

Silence would take over the entire house. After Mom finished cleaning up, there would then be complete silence. That seemed to be the signal for my father to say his line to Mom. Clearing his throat, he would ask:

"Are you ready?"

It didn't matter how Mom responded, what she said or did, the tone of her voice, her body language, facial expressions, her complaints, nothing mattered. Mom was going to be beaten almost every night around 8 p.m. Sometimes she would reluctantly go to my father, moving slowly. He would stare at her for a moment.

Slap!

He would usually start the beating by slapping her face, hard.

Slap! Slap!

If she raised her hands to cover her face, then he would punch her in another part of her body, usually her stomach. If she didn't leave the kitchen fast enough, then he would grab her by the hair, arm, or shirt, drag her to the living room and beat her there. At other times, he would start throwing things at her. A broom or dustpan, or whatever he could grab, he would throw it to officially start the beat-down. Then he would beat her until he was tired, and he didn't tire easily. Punching, slapping, kicking. His fists and feet were his primary weapons. Sometimes he would throw her against the wall in the living room.

When he was beating Mom, I wished I could be bigger or that someone could come to stop it. I was just three years old, a little girl who was increasingly terrified of her father and crying for her mother.

If he had meant to kill Mom, he could have done so easily. My father towered over her. He was a giant by North Korean standards. Generations after the country was established in 1948, North Koreans are reportedly three to four inches shorter than South Koreans. My father was an exception, about 5'11" tall, physically fit, tough. Mom was nine inches shorter, and no match for him. She would grab his clothes trying to hold on to stop his punches, slaps, and kicks.

Being an active tomboy, I would try to stop my father from beating Mom. However, I was as threatening as a newborn puppy growling at a burglar. I would grab my father's right leg as he was hitting Mom, holding on so at least he couldn't kick her.

"Please, stop... don't hurt my Mommy!" I would look up at my father, with my body wrapped around his leg, pleading with my eyes for him to stop. He was hitting Mom, but he wasn't showing anger. He was as emotionless as a farmer cutting off the head of another chicken.

Mom would say, as a command, "Songmi-ya, go to your grandmother." My name is Songmi, which means "pine tree." The "ah" or "ya," depending on if a name ends in a vowel or consonant, was the ending that Koreans, both North and South, attach to the ending of words. It shows closeness, but also hierarchy, with an older or elder person using that ending for younger people. As a North Korean child, I was taught at home to obey my parents, and in preschool I was taught to worship the dictators and their family members.

Mom was dodging and absorbing blows, but she was worried that her little baby would be injured. I couldn't understand how my father could be so mean. I pled, through tears and sobs, to Grandma Bae, "Please stop my daddy."

Sometimes Grandma Bae would try to stop him, but to no avail. He would easily push her out of the way. "Stop! Get over there!" he would shout, glaring at my grandma. "Don't try to stop me!" It was a rare time that he showed emotion; it was a rare time that anyone in the home challenged him.

I would try to hide so I didn't have to watch. Our home was big by North Korean standards. We had a kitchen, living room and two bedrooms, and nearby we had a storage room and an outside toilet. In addition, for the many animals our family raised, we had a chicken coop, a pigsty, a doghouse, a rabbit house, and an area for goats.

The home was big, but when my father was beating Mom, it seemed so small at that moment. No matter how far away I tried to get from the beatings, it still seemed that I was right there next to Mom as she was being beaten. Doing as I had been told, I would retreat to the living room, crying, sitting on the floor, holding onto my grandma's legs.

Uncle Gicheol would be there sometimes, but he was the younger brother. I didn't know then that they were stepbrothers and that I wasn't related to Uncle Gicheol or Grandma Bae by blood. Sick with tuberculosis, he was so skinny, pale, and weak. Anyone who saw him could tell that he was sick. He would try to stop his older and stronger stepbrother, but he was too weak physically.

He was almost the same height as my father, but he

looked like a skeleton. One day, as my father was beating Mom, my uncle grabbed my father's wrist to stop him from throwing another punch. It was a good athletic move, especially for a frail man, but it was like grabbing a tiger by the tail. On that occasion, my uncle looked directly into my father's eyes, trying to reason with him, "Big Brother. Please stop it."

In response, my father aggressively grabbed his arm, threatening but not hitting his sick brother. "Don't intervene. This is not your business."

My uncle was too weak to fight; we all knew he didn't have the energy or strength to stop my father. He tried at times, but he was usually missing 15 minutes before 8 p.m. He was a witness to frequent beatings that he was helpless to stop. In North Korea, the police are more interested in punishing people who have said something negative or damaged the likeness or reputation of the North Korean dictators. Beating a spouse was something for the family to work out.

Mom would cover her face to try to block my father's punches and slaps, but he easily broke through her weak defense. When Mom fell, it seemed the entire universe had collapsed. My father would kick Mom as she was curled up in the fetal position. There was nothing she could do about a big man determined to beat her up. He rarely spoke as he beat her. What terrified me most of all was his silence. He rarely spoke around the home, his mind always seemed to be somewhere else. He rarely talked during the beatings so Mom couldn't argue with him because he didn't respond.

I wanted to comfort Mom, to hug her, but she would be in pain and have a knee-jerk response to touches. Mom often couldn't sleep at night because of the pain. She wouldn't leave home because her face was red and blue from the constant beatings.

My father's favorite place to beat Mom was in the living room. I had been an active rough-and-tumble tomboy laughing at everything, but I was turning into a crybaby. My father didn't care about Mom's pain, grandma's protests, uncle's reasoning, or my tears.

Those beatings are among my first memories in life. I have near-photographic memory about things from the age of three. Apparently, the trauma woke up my brain early. I can remember things in detail; I am unable to forget them even when I try. My father's flat statement before a beating still rings in my ears today.

"Are you ready?"

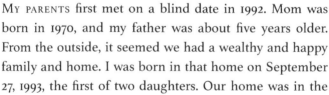

MY PARENTS first met on a blind date in 1992. Mom was born in 1970, and my father was about five years older. From the outside, it seemed we had a wealthy and happy family and home. I was born in that home on September 27, 1993, the first of two daughters. Our home was in the Geumya-gun, Bongsan-ri area that is in the middle of North Korea.

It was during the peak of North Korea's famine of the 1990s. There are estimates that, out of North Korea's population of about 25 million people, about 500,000 to 3 million starved to death. In a country where many were starving to death or eating grass to survive, having a dinner table with numerous dishes full of food meant you were affluent.

Despite that seemingly good situation, the marriage of

my parents was doomed almost from the beginning. There were three main factors that led to the breakup.

The first factor was the death of my paternal grandfather. I later learned that my father had previously been in a relationship with a woman that he really wanted to marry. In North Korea at that time, people did not marry out of love. Marriages were typically arranged by parents. My father, however, had found the woman he wanted to be with.

His own father had objected to the marriage, and as a loyal son, my father had to accept his own father's objection. My grandfather had opposed the relationship because the other woman had the same family name. "Han" is not as common of a family name as Kim, Lee and Park in North Korea. Times may have changed somewhat, but as late as the 1990s, it was still forbidden by many families for a Han to marry someone with the Han family name. If you meet another Han, you assume that you are related in some way. Whereas, Kim, Lee and Park family names have many ancestral lines, the Han family has only one line. A Han marrying another person with the Han family name was out of the question for older North Koreans.

Even after being married for several years, my father wanted that other woman. As a loyal son, he obeyed his father's wishes. Then, everything changed after his father died. The loyal son no longer had to abide by his late father's wishes. My father began meeting that other woman again. He never showed emotion with our family, and his mind always seemed to be preoccupied, away from his family. He may not have felt love with his family, but apparently, he did know what love was with the other woman. Marriage to Mom had not ended his feelings for his first love. His father's death gave him an opportunity to rekindle his old flame.

Mom knew about the other woman, but initially she didn't protest or complain. There is a saying in Korean that sometimes it is better not to know. A person will ignore what his or her spouse is doing for the sake of keeping a marriage together.

The second factor that led to the breakup of the family was even more serious than a husband having a mistress: my baby sister died when she was just a year old.

I don't remember the exact day or month, but I think it might have been in May of 1997. I remember that it was raining so hard that day. My sister and I attended the preschool that was about a five-minute walk from home. Like other children, my baby sister and I started preschool at the age of one.

On that day, however, I was alone. After lunch but before the regular nap time, the teachers were washing the dishes, organizing things, and talking together. I overheard one of them say, "Oh, no. Seolmi died." Seolmi had been sick that morning, but there was no way she could be dead. I wanted to go home, but I was too young to leave on my own. I was looking out the window, listening to the heavy rain hitting the ground, quietly crying.

At home, my stunned family members were all crying. Grandma Bae had cooked dinner in a daze, but it didn't matter because no one ate. I later heard the rest of the story of what happened that terrible day. My sister had looked fine when we were getting ready for preschool that morning. After changing her diaper, Mom picked up Seolmi. My sister began screaming in pain. Mom was startled. Babies sometimes cry, but this was different. She noticed that Seolmi's lower body was bright red. When Mom touched her again, Seolmi started screaming again.

Alarmed, Mom sprang into action. She alerted the family that something was wrong. She asked Grandma Bae to walk me to preschool then my parents got prepared to take Seolmi to the clinic that was about a 15-minute walk away. Because it was so early in the morning, they first went to the home of the doctor who was the clinic's director.

The doctor was there, but he said they needed to go to a bigger hospital about two hours away. My parents both ran and walked, with Seolmi strapped to Mom's back. They approached the hospital, but Seolmi wasn't breathing. They arrived at the hospital, frantic. The doctor and nurses tried to revive her, but it was too late. My baby sister had already died.

It was unbelievable. We had been playing together the day before and had breakfast together that morning. My father began beating Mom after Seolmi's death. My father loved my little sister so much. Friends and family members would say that Seolmi resembled my father, even her voice sounded like his. It seemed that I was Mom's daughter and Seolmi was my father's daughter.

My father blamed Mom for Seolmi's death. He had already been a bit aloof with the family. After Seolmi's death, he often blamed Mom for not noticing sooner that Seolmi was sick. Whatever problems they were already having were exacerbated by Seolmi's sudden death.

The third factor that led to the implosion of my family: Mom's side of the family began struggling financially. My father's side of the family was well-off as my paternal grandfather had a huge home and was influential. Mom's side of the family had been doing well, but then my maternal grandparents both suffered strokes and my maternal grandfather died.

I have no memory of my maternal grandfather. I only remember one photo of him that Mom showed me after I asked about him. He was sitting alone in a chair. I noticed there was a problem with his eyes. I asked directly: "What's wrong with his eyes?" They were white, one eye was closed. I also noticed that the index and middle fingers on his right hand were missing. He had been a hero during the Korean War, losing two fingers during the fighting and also losing his vision.

The government gave him some money every month to reward his war valor. North Korea is one big military, and soldiers and war heroes were rewarded. Mom's mother, Grandma Choi, had been making some money selling medicine, and my grandfather's stipend added to their income. But there were too many people in the home—seven in all—to live on their money.

Grandma Choi suffered a stroke. They sold medicine to pay for her medical expenses. As she was getting better, my grandfather suffered a stroke. The treatment of both grandparents bankrupted the family. North Korea's medical system is "free," but doctors must be bribed when higher-level treatment was needed. Both grandparents were sick, but they had run out of money, the government wasn't paying much, and they didn't have enough food.

Every day my grandfather was saying, "I'm hungry. I'm so hungry. I need to eat." They had run out of money and food. My grandfather, the war hero, the leader of Mom's family, starved to death.

After his death, Mom's relatives struggled even more. My maternal grandma was getting better, then she suffered another stroke. Mom's youngest sister, Aunt

Yeonhui, was a high school student then; she had started selling food she had cooked. Desperate, she and other members of Mom's family went to my father to ask for help.

That seemed to drive my father over the edge. He was secretly meeting his mistress, was angry about the death of his younger daughter, and now the wife he was abusing had relatives asking him for help.

Mom was also fed up, and not just because of the beatings. She knew her husband had money and could share with her relatives, but he rejected them in person. She wanted to help her family as they tried to survive from one shock after another. A North Korean woman should not challenge her husband's authority, but Mom began to do so. She knew he was meeting another woman, but she hadn't said anything at first. Finally, she informed him that she knew he had a mistress, that she knew who the other woman was. She said she would be fine if he lived with that other woman.

With the beatings getting worse, my father's refusal to help Mom's relatives, and with him continuing to meet the other woman, Mom finally said she wanted to get divorced. In North Korea, both sides must agree to a divorce. My father had started meeting the other woman, but he didn't want to get divorced. At that time, it was shameful for a family to have a divorce in it. My father wanted both a wife and a mistress. My family looked successful, but Mom was about to shatter that facade by trying to get divorced.

Finally, Mom left. She went to Grandma Choi's home, battered and bruised. I later learned that my father visited Mom to ask her to reconcile. Mom's response was simple: "We're finished." She wasn't going to be beaten again, she knew that her husband wanted another woman, she was tired of getting blamed for their daughter's death, and she knew he wasn't interested in helping her family. My father may have wanted to reconcile because he didn't want to break up the family.

After Mom left, I was living with my father, uncle, and Grandma Bae. My father was expecting Mom to return. One reason is that her family was poor. Their desperate situation had gotten even worse. It seemed logical that Mom would miss the affluence of my father's home. We had plenty to eat unlike at Grandma Choi's home.

A second reason that he expected her to return is that Mom and I were very close. At some point, the mother would certainly return to her surviving daughter. Third, Mom initially had been willing to accept that her husband had a mistress. At some point, like other wives of wealthy men in North Korea, she might have been willing to accept the arrangement. It made sense that my father thought Mom would return. But then days turned into weeks, then it was three months, and there was no sign that Mom would return.

It was a lonely time for me. I was just a child, so I couldn't know all of the circumstances of what was going on in the family. I felt like I didn't have a family. I was living with my father, uncle and grandma, but it was Mom who I wanted to be with. I loved my grandma, but no one could compare with Mom.

My father had not changed. There were no beatings, so it almost became a normal home. However, I had an uncomfortable feeling when I was alone with him. He didn't smile. He didn't talk much. After work, he would return home, eat dinner, watch TV, smoke. Then he would go to sleep at around 8:30 or 9:00 p.m.

~

I DID LOVE the home I was born into. Before the breakup, life had its wonderful moments. I woke up jumping out of bed. I wanted to go outside to talk to the animals even before getting dressed. My favorites were the dogs and goats. Sometimes I would go with my grandma to feed the goats; I really loved watching them eat grass. They would be moving their whole faces as they were eating. Sometimes I would try to show them how to eat, pretending I was chewing something. I hoped they would learn by watching me, but they never did. The goats seemed to be moving the grass from one side of their mouths to the other, unlike humans who bite and chew up and down.

"Grandma, look at the goats. Their whole faces are moving."

"Little one, are you looking at their faces?" my grandma responded. "Is it funny?"

"Yes!" I said as we laughed together.

I loved goat milk, so after I learned where the milk came from, I wanted to help milk the goats. The little tomboy wasn't content to just watch. After milking them, my grandma and I would boil the milk. I loved having goat milk with rice. I was a picky eater then. My grandma was always trying to feed me different kinds of food, especially meat, fish and soup. I usually refused to eat meat; I didn't even want to look at it. I didn't know that many North Koreans were starving at that time and would have happily died while eating meat.

There was only one kind of fish that I enjoyed: flatfish. I didn't eat kimchi, and most of all, I didn't enjoy soybean paste stew, which is a favorite of many North Koreans. My family being affluent, I could be picky because there was always more food to choose from.

"That's smelly, I don't want to eat," I often said. I smelled food first, leaning over, like a picky dog sniffing. I could always come up with a reason that I didn't want to eat or drink something, but I never turned down goat milk.

Then next, I would visit the pigs to watch Grandma Bae feed them. I often stood on my tippy toes trying to look inside the pigsty. I loved the dogs and goats, but I teased the pigs.

"I don't like you, Pig. You are so dirty and pooping everywhere. Oh, smelly!" I often held my nose in case the pigs couldn't understand what I was saying. Surely the pigs would understand my body language.

They would rub up against the wall to scratch an itch. I wondered: "Are pigs ticklish? Itchy?" They would be trying so hard to scratch their itches, and I would be laughing so hard. They would rub up against the gate or anything else to cause friction.

"GRANDMA!" I was constantly calling for my grandma. At times, our home and entire area seemed to be filled with my voice calling out: "GRANDMA!"

"Yes?"

"Why are they scratching? Can I help them?"

She handed me a stick, then showed me how to scratch the pigs. Using the stick, I started scratching the backs and stomachs of the pigs. The pigs would come to me, seeming to know that I enjoyed it as much as they did. One pig was waiting, inviting me to scratch his stomach. I did so, and he loved it. From that time, I would scratch their itches as part of the feeding process.

"Hey Pig, are you happy now?"

I felt at one with the animals and was constantly trying to communicate with them.

"Grandma! Can they understand me? I can't understand them." I tried making the oink sounds that pigs make. Maybe they could understand me if I spoke their language. I had seen Grandma Bae calling the chickens by making a "goo goo, goo goo, goo googoo" sound. I thought my grandma knew the chicken language. I began making the sound with the chickens.

The chickens were coming to me! Just like that, I had become a fluent Chicken Language speaker. Having quickly mastered the Chicken Language, I then wanted to become a fluent Pig Language speaker.

Around our home, we had many fruit trees. After I learned to count, one of the first things I wanted to count was the fruit trees around our home. There were 24 in all, which I confirmed almost every day when I was outside with Grandma Bae to feed the animals and scratch the pigs. If a tree ever disappeared, I would have known it, because I would have counted them the day before.

To Grandma Bae, I could do nothing wrong, no matter how many times I called her name, asking her to do this and that, to explain this or that, that I didn't want to eat this or that. There was only love from her.

I was happy at that big house, with so many animals and fruit trees. Serene would have been the word to use, as I was at one with the animals and trees. I would stare at the animals, wondering, "What are they thinking. Are they happy? How are they communicating with each other? What are they seeing when they look at us? Is the grass yummy?"

It was all so wonderful, until dinner time. After Mom

left home, even those outings with Grandma Bae were not as much fun.

I was more careful, quieter after Mom left. After three months, I told my father that I missed Mom. I finally found the courage to ask him directly. "Why can't I see her?" The question had been on my mind every day. I could say anything to Mom and Grandma Bae, but I would think first before talking to my father. I had even learned to be careful talking about him to others. He had been a scary man beating Mom.

He didn't answer immediately. A bit later, he said to Grandma Bae, "Mom, bring me Songmi's clothes."

"What? It is so late already. You can't go out now."

"I can go anywhere." He did what he wanted to do. Everything was a command, even to his stepmother. Grandma Bae must have known that he wouldn't listen to her. Every conversation was one way, from his direction. There was never any back-and-forth conversation with him, only assertions, statements, commands, and orders from him.

More casual than usual, he said to me: "Okay, let's go see your mom."

Grandma Bae probably guessed what he was planning to do. As directed, Grandma Bae got my clothes. Getting dressed with my grandma was usually fun, but I could see that her usually cheerful face was serious and sad. Although we had shared many happy times, the look on her face at that moment was one I will never forget.

Tears were rolling down my grandma's cheeks as she got me dressed. I was confused. It was a happy moment because I was going to see Mom. My father still didn't seem to have a heart, but at least he wasn't being violent.

Maybe this meant that Mom could come back with us, and we could live together again.

"Grandma, why are you crying?"

"Nothing," she said. "I hope you can be happy with your mom. Please eat well."

Eating well had never been a problem, even for a picky eater. As we said goodbye, Grandma Bae tried not to cry as my father looked on. I had mixed feelings of joy at seeing Mom but sadness at saying goodbye to my grandma.

We started down a long dirt road leading from our home. Although it was a father-and-daughter out walking together late at night, we weren't walking hand in hand. I was a young girl who didn't have any special feelings about her father.

We walked. And walked and walked and walked. I started wondering how long it was going to take. This was the countryside of North Korea; it was tough to get around. It would be several years before I would ride in a car. For a long time, I didn't know people could have personal vehicles; that seemed to be something reserved for government officials. If we had been important people, we could have had a car, my baby sister could have lived because my parents could have rushed her to the hospital, and it is possible that our family would not have broken up. At least, not at that time. And without the nightly violence.

It was so dark and scary walking late at night. Where I grew up in North Korea, the streetlights were used only to light up the statues of the dictators of North Korea. At night, you had to feel your way around or rely on your memory. There weren't homes with lights to show you the way. Usually, there was no electricity at night. Most of the year, we would use candles and many families would use tree limbs that were basically fire lit on a stick. But it was so irritating if you used that during the night. In the morning, when you washed your face, you would be like a chimney, blowing dust and soot out of your nose.

North Korea was a dark country at night. And the dark was a reason not to be out late at night, as my father and I were that night. My father was walking so fast I had to run to keep up with him. I couldn't see any lights; I was running to keep up with my father. "Dad, I'm so scared."

That would have been a moment for a father to hold his daughter's hand, to give her a hug, to reassure her in some way. "Don't worry," he said. "You will see your mom."

Everything I said, my father responded that I would be seeing Mom soon. He was not angry, there was no excitement in his voice. On the other hand, I was so excited that I would get to see Mom again, but I could sense that I should not express excitement. First, however, we had more walking to do.

"How long do we have to go?" I asked, still running to keep up with my father. He was so tall, his legs looked even longer as he hurried.

"Over there," he replied. I finally smiled, knowing we were getting closer. I asked again how long it would take. Pointing, he said, "Do you see that light?" In the far distance, I could see a small light.

"Your mother isn't sleeping yet. You will meet her soon, and you can live with her from now on," he said.

I was so exhausted that I didn't grasp the full meaning or implication. *You can live with her from now on.* Would we be living together? Were we all going to stay together in Grandma Choi's home? I couldn't figure out his exact meaning, and I was too exhausted to figure it out. Finally, I kind of collapsed on the ground. He didn't get frustrated or angry. He picked me up and carried me on his back, sprinting. I was so tired that I fell asleep on his back, even as he sprinted at top speed.

Around midnight, we arrived. We had run and walked for five hours, mostly sprinting by my father. I woke up to see that the small light was now very close. When we arrived at the door, my father said, "Okay, you can go in."

Even as he was preparing to dump me out of his life, he couldn't say my name, he didn't comfort me, he didn't hug or kiss his scared young daughter, he didn't even say goodbye. He just said: "Okay, you can go in."

Not looking back at my father, I knocked on the door.

2

HOME, SWEET...BARN

M om and Grandma Choi were so surprised when they opened the door to see me. After being apart for months, I was suddenly at their door far from home.

"How did you get here?" In just five seconds, I felt more love and concern than I had in the previous three months with my father, probably more than during all of my years with him. Aunt Yeonhui also greeted me. She had been cooking, getting ready for the next day to sell food on the street. I explained that my father had brought me there but that he had left immediately.

Grandma Choi was paralyzed on the left side of her body after suffering a second stroke. She was worried about my father because it was already late. He would have to go a long distance at night, arriving home at about 5 a.m.

Aunt Yeonhui disagreed. "He can rest at his home." She didn't want him to come in. When my grandparents were suffering from health problems, my father rejected the desperate plea from my mom's family as he sat in his huge home. He wouldn't want or expect Aunt Yeonhui's help now.

"I know him," Mom said. "He won't come in." He needed to return to his castle, where he was the dictator. At the home of his estranged wife's family, he would be a visitor and an unwelcome one. Surely, he wouldn't feel comfortable; in addition to rejecting their pleas for help, they would know that he had been beating Mom and had a mistress. He wouldn't want to sit in their home; he'd prefer to walk or run for hours rather than having to show gratitude as a guest.

They embraced me, then we had some nice fruit. After that, I fell asleep in Mom's arms.

SIX MONTHS after Mom started the divorce, it became final. Although my parents had gotten divorced, I saw my father very often for a few years. In North Korea at that time, it wasn't easy to move around without government permission and it wasn't easy to get that permission. It isn't easy to go to another province without permission; it isn't easy to move to a different home.

Mom started making plans to leave. One reason is that there simply wasn't enough food to feed everyone in the house (my grandma, Mom, two aunts, uncle, and me). A second reason is that we needed to be back in the Bongsan-ri region when our new home from the government became available. Mom's address was still registered as being in my father's home, and we were waiting to get permission to move. A third reason: Mom needed to start working again. It was time for a new start. Mom and her other sister, Aunt Seonhui, loaded up various household items such as bowls, blankets, pillows, clothes, and cooking tools onto a handcart. Aunt Seonhui would help us with the move before returning to Grandma Choi's home the next day. My Uncle Geumcheol was out, as usual, probably drinking, chatting with friends, or collecting wood.

I was scared as Mom and Aunt Seonhui began pulling the handcart to leave Grandma Choi's home to go back to Bongsan-ri. My heart was pounding with every step, unsure of exactly what was going to happen to us. At first, I was walking with them. Aunt Seonhui then had an idea: "Songmi-ya, can you help us push the cart?" I think I saw her smiling, or was it a smirk on her face? But then she looked serious.

"Of course!" I was probably four years old. Mom and Aunt Seonhui were pulling the handcart, and I was pushing from behind.

"Songmi-ya, are you pushing hard?"

"Yes, I am!"

Aunt Seonhui and Mom couldn't control their laughter. "We can't feel you pushing."

"Mom, Aunt." I came from behind the cart. "My face is so red, and I am sweating so much." I wiped the sweat off my brow to make sure they could see how much I was sweating. They laughed even harder. "Mom, Aunt, don't tease me! I was pushing so hard!"

"You are like a cute ant," Mom said, still laughing. "We couldn't feel you pushing." We were in a terrible situation, struggling to drag that handcart such a long distance. At that moment, I didn't see anything funny. "My stomach hurts from laughing," Mom said.

Ignoring them, I resumed pushing from behind the handcart. After more pushing, I got tired and needed to take a break. "Mom, I can't walk anymore. My feet hurt. I'm sleepy."

Mom had still been giggling, but then she got serious. "I have an idea. Can you get on the handcart?"

"Really? Can I?" The cart didn't look that comfortable, but it still looked like it could be fun to ride on it. Aunt Seonhui picked me up and put me on the handcart. This was going to be more fun than pushing the cart. "Sit here?" I asked.

"No. Move over a little."

They had thought I was useless when I was pushing the cart, but now it seemed that I was valuable. Some of the items had shifted as the handcart was being dragged. They needed me to balance the cart with my weight. I fell asleep almost immediately. It felt so comfortable. Then Aunt Seonhui woke me up. My body had tipped over. "Songmi-ya, if you move to a different position then it becomes more difficult for us to pull the cart," Aunt Seonhui said gently but firmly. Their laughter had turned to seriousness. They wanted me to be comfortable, but there was the reality of them struggling more.

I was rubbing my eyes to stay awake. "Mom, I'm hungry, how much longer do we have to go?" She gave the bad news. We had only gone about halfway. We had gone about five hours. "That's too long," I said. They were probably thinking the same thing. Then they got hungry, too. A bit later, we came upon some places selling snacks on the road. They bought some food, and we ate. After that, Mom and Aunt Seonhui said they were tired. I was happy because I was with Mom. I was happy no matter what we were doing when we were together; I always felt comfortable with her. Of my two aunts, I preferred Aunt Seonhui. She was so kind, unlike Aunt Yeonhui who was a bit cold.

We were walking on a dirt road, so it was uncomfortable pushing and pulling the cart. Whenever a car passed by, there was so much dust that we couldn't see. If a car was coming by, Mom would warn, "Songmi-ya, don't breathe."

I was born at a time known in North Korea as the "Arduous March". I had been living a life of luxury, but now we were having an arduous march of our own. Even some wealthy families were struggling to survive — what would happen to us? I started to worry when I began wondering about our destination. "Mom, where are we going?"

Aunt Seonhui answered, "You don't know? You are going back near your father's house." I had mixed feelings. I was happy to go there because I could see Grandma Bae and my friends, but I was afraid of my father. "Where are we going to live?"

Mom answered, "We aren't sure exactly." Despite the uncertainty, I was happy. I could see the contrast between Mom and my father. The last time I had seen him, my father had walked fast and then sprinted for hours so he could dump me out of his life and start a new family. In contrast, Mom, Aunt Seonhui and I slowly pushed and pulled the handcart for 10 hours knowing that Mom and I would be alone in the world.

My father had barely acknowledged my existence, barely talked, and dismissed my questions by telling me that I would be able to see my mom. In contrast, Mom and I were truly together, walking and talking together as mother and daughter, and also in good spirits because Aunt Seonhui had joined us. Even having them tease me was fun because I knew they loved me. They were laughing so much; it was like going on a fun family trip. Our move was during the daytime instead of the scary night, we weren't in a hurry, and we were having fun despite the difficult trip. And the final contrast: my father had returned to a nice house. Mom, Aunt Seonhui and I arrived at our destination: a barn.

THE BARN MOM and I were moving to was even smaller than the storage room at my father's home. Our lives had been turned upside down since the death of my baby sister. Now we had come to this moment. We opened the dirty old door to the barn, and Mom quickly concluded we couldn't stay there that night. There seemed to be only three things inside: dust, dirt, and rice straw. It was already late, we hadn't eaten for a few hours, and we were so tired.

As a barn, it might have been perfectly fine. It was not appropriate for humans, however. It wasn't exactly home, sweet home. It was our best option at that moment. It was going to be our housing until we were assigned to another home by local officials.

Near the barn was the main building of the orchard manager. Mom asked if we could stay in the office that night. We were in a bad situation, reduced to living in a barn, but Mom had to draw the line somewhere about what we could tolerate. She would continue trying to maintain our dignity as human beings, although it would get more difficult in the coming years.

Mom had worked with the manager before, so there was some familiarity. The manager was probably in his 50s, skinny and short. He was willing to allow us to stay in the office that night, although of course we couldn't expect that kind of thing long-term. The office felt so good, so warm. We slept there that night. I snuggled up to Mom, wondering what would happen to us. I looked into Mom's eyes, and she looked into mine. We didn't say anything at that moment, but I said to myself: "I am going to be with my Mommy forever." I would always be a good daughter to her, to thank her for bringing me into the world.

This was going to be the start of our new lives. We were relying on an orchard guard to allow us to stay in a barn. At that moment, we were grateful for even that. What would have happened to us without even that barn? North Korea didn't seem to be the heaven that I had learned about in my preschool classes.

The next morning under the sun, we got a look at the barn. It had been too dirty for us to stay in the night before. We had kept our dignity by not sleeping there that first night. Now we would need to make it suitable for humans. Mom sprang into action. It would take about a week to make the repairs and upgrades. She was always finding a way to survive through every situation.

Because it would be a week before we could move into the barn, the orchard manager asked if we could stay in a hut overlooking the orchard. It wasn't just out of benevolence. His orchard was a target for people stealing food. North Korea had been going through a famine, so it was common for many people to steal food.

There were no lights in the hut, making it very dark, but at least it wasn't dirty like the barn. When it rained, Mom and I would sit together, trying to avoid getting wet in that cold, uncomfortable hut.

"My baby, are your feet cold?" She placed my feet between her thighs to keep them warm. Mom would sleep on her side, hugging me, her arm my pillow. The hut was so small, and that was okay for me because I was so small. Even at 5'2", Mom's legs were too long for the hut. She could not stretch out her legs because the hut wasn't big enough. Mom cooked outside, using a small bowl. It would get so cold at night, and we didn't have enough blankets. She never complained about our situation; she did her best to make things comfortable for me. I will never forget that time. I developed a lifelong love for Mom. She was truly the center of my universe.

During the day, Mom was at the barn helping with repairs. About 20 minutes away, I stayed at the hut over-looking the orchard. The guard had mentioned there were many people coming to steal vegetables. Being four years old, there was nothing I could do to stop food thieves. As the daughter of a single mom, I was growing up in a hurry.

I asked Mom, "What should I do if someone comes to steal something?"

"You should pretend to call me." So that was the plan. I was to be an actress, trying to fool the vegetable thieves into thinking I wasn't alone. It didn't take long for the scenario to come true. I saw some people walking around the vegetables. They were looking around with one eye on the vegetables and another eye looking to see if there was anyone around to catch them.

"MOM!" I screamed! "I'M HUNGRY! Are you cooking now?" The eyes of the two women widened when they saw me. They had been caught in the act. Their legs were frozen. The older one asked, "Is your mom here?"

"YES!" I was nervous and terrified. I wanted them to think I was angry. As they got closer, I could see that the younger one was actually a young girl, probably a teenager. They were not dressed nicely. They might have been a mother and daughter, or two women who had come together to support each other. Suddenly, I felt so thankful that at least Mom and I could stay at this hut. The older woman spoke again. She asked directly: "Could you give us some cucumbers? Just two. We don't want to steal." But this didn't mean they wouldn't. They were so hungry that they didn't try to strike up a conversation. They could have fled, but that would have meant searching around for another food target. I was only a little girl, so they could have taken what they wanted. Perhaps they wanted to maintain some dignity and not steal from a little girl.

Almost as soon as I handed her the cucumbers, the older woman grabbed them with her rough hands and gave one to the young girl with her. They were greedily and shamelessly eating cucumbers handed to them by a child. They both thanked me, the older woman handing me a nice hair clip. Perhaps it felt like bartering rather than begging by giving me something.

AFTER ONE WEEK of repairs done by the orchard staff, the barn was as ready as it was going to be for humans. It had been so long since the barn had been heated, it probably forgot how to be warm. Despite the upgrades, the barn looked poor. It was poor. We were poor. There was only one small room and a very small area for the kitchen. The table was in the middle of the barn, which was the place for everything. Mom and I would sit across from each other as we ate. The door was to the left of my seat. The small kitchen area was next to the door. There was no barrier or wall. There was a small window behind Mom's seat. There was not enough space in the barn to sleep comfortably.

There is a Korean saying: "Even if the sky falls, there is a hole to escape." That is, no matter how bad things look, there's always a solution. That seemed to be true with Mom. There were so many times that it was difficult to survive. No house, no food, but she always found a way. I always felt that Mom was trying to make my life as comfortable as possible. She would only eat vegetables and try to make sure I had some grains and something solid to eat. She couldn't give me an affluent home, but she would give me the best of what she had.

I had gone from living in my father's wonderful house with all kinds of farm animals and food to living in a hut and then a barn. From the barn, I could see my father's house in the distance. He was living in a different world. Even though he was a cold person, his home was warm and cozy with Grandma Bae and so many animals. Compared to the barn and the hut, it seemed like my father was living in a grand palace.

Grandma Bae and neighbors would sometimes bring food to us. My father could probably guess what was happening to us, but he didn't offer us any help. My parents had divorced, and for my father, that apparently meant the end of his association with me. And that's what it felt like — an association, not a true family connection.

One day, I came home early after preschool. Mom was at work, and I was bored. I used to play with grandma or uncle or feed the animals after preschool. Suddenly, I thought, "I will go see my grandma now." I was worried that Mom would get angry. "Nobody knows I am going. I will keep the secret to myself."

My father's house had a big door. I knocked on the door, "Grandma!" The dog barked whenever a stranger knocked on the door, but her tail was wagging like crazy. She was whining and scratching, trying to get to me.

"Grandma!"

I saw that her hands were wet, she was shaking them to get the water off. "Come in!"

I was laughing again. "I missed you!"

Grandma Bae looked so happy, but also sad. She hugged me for a long time. "How are you doing? How is the barn? Are you eating well? What are you eating?"

"Grandma, why don't you come see me?"

"Sweetie, I missed you so much, but I can't go to see you because of your father and stepmother." I went inside and laid down, it felt like my house. I had been born in that house, taken my first steps in that house, become aware of the world when I was in that house. I took off my shoes, ran around like I had in the past when I was a playful, innocent little girl throwing pillows at Uncle Gicheol. It seemed like old times that weren't that long ago. She gave me some rice and side dishes. She was firing questions at me. "Grandma, I'm so hungry, I can't think."

It was the early afternoon, so no one else was home. I was happy to have my face licked by the dog again. "Oh no, don't scratch me!" The dog was so happy to see me. "Grandma, I really miss this house, but I should not come here. Mom doesn't know that I came here."

"Of course, me too, I can't let your father and step-mother know." It was almost 6 p.m. I knew my father would be returning soon.

"Songmi-ya, you need to go, I need to cook for them."

"Okay, can I come sometimes?"

"Of course, but please be careful. Your stepmother might get angry."

"Grandma, I know what you mean." I was young, but I was aware of the adult battles that had destroyed our family. Both Grandma Bae and I were both so sad when I left.

A few days later, I decided to visit my grandmother again. I could see my grandma through the window. Then I saw the face of another woman. I guessed that it might be my new stepmother. The dog started whining, scratching. The woman came to check. "Is there somebody there?"

I knew I needed to be careful, but I had not prepared to hide myself. I froze. She saw me. I quietly said my name.

She was shorter than Mom and not as beautiful as Mom. She had small eyes, unlike Mom's big, beautiful eyes. I was wondering why my father loved that ugly woman who had an angry look on her face. My father always had a frown on his face, so instead of a smiling woman like Mom, he must have preferred a woman who also had a permanent frown on her face. She responded: "Why are you here?"

My new stepmother wasn't even interested in seeing if she could be a mom to me. Anyway, I wasn't there to see her or my father. "I miss my grandma. Can I come in?"

She was scowling, but she said, "Sure, you can."

It wasn't comfortable. My grandma looked at my stepmother. My stepmother was looking back at her, glaring. I couldn't be sure what was going on. I could guess that I wasn't welcome. Biting my lip, I said, "Grandma, I'm going to go home." I didn't want to go, I wanted a few more minutes with my lovely grandma.

For the first time, my stepmother showed something besides an icy glare. "Are you going? You can have dinner with us." It was probably very painful for her to say those words that she must not have meant. I wanted it, but I was thinking about Mom. Grandma Bae said, "You can stay."

A short time later, my father came in. He hadn't seen me in a while, but he hadn't changed. "You're here?" He could have welcomed me as his daughter. But it was more like he was noticing the time of the day, not that his daughter was there. He didn't say anything after that. My stepmother was also silent. It felt so uncomfortable. I ate dinner with them at the same dinner table grandma and I had dominated just months before. But now, I was an unwelcome guest, a trespasser. It was time for me to leave. I felt unwelcome, and I knew that Mom might have been searching for me.

My stepmother came out with me. She had done her best to look friendly during dinner, but at every moment, I still felt like a big dog was ready to bite me. Once outside, my stepmother was blunt: "Never come back."

After my stepmother went in, I pointed at the house: "I'm never coming back. You can eat everything, you can live a better life. One day you are going to regret this." With that, I began walking back to the barn, wondering what would happen there if Mom was waiting for me.

I HAD BEEN unwelcome at my former home, and now I was probably going to be in trouble at the barn. Mom was cooking dinner. It was going to be grass again. "Mom." I said it softly.

She turned to look at me. "Where were you?"

Speaking slowly and evasively, I tried not to admit where I had been. "Did you have dinner with them? I was looking for you everywhere." She had asked my friends if they knew where I was. They hadn't seen me. There was one place she couldn't check, so she guessed that's where I had been. I confessed that I had been at our old home.

Mom was angry, but her curiosity won out first. "What did your stepmother say? How's your father? And your grandmother?" I was telling the truth slowly. I told her everything verbatim, starting with the dog seeing me, my stepmother spotting me then inviting me to come in, that I got to play with the animals again, that my father came in, then we had dinner. I was leaving out the bad ending.

"Did your stepmother say anything else?" There was no wiggle room for me to evade. I was wondering if I should repeat my stepmother's final statement. I had motioned at the home and said that I would never return, but I knew that if Mom heard what my stepmother said, she would also order me never to return. With my head bowed, I said, "She said for me to never come back."

"See!" For the first time, Mom really got angry about my trip back home. "Never go back. That is not your father anymore. That is not your mother. That is not your house anymore."

"What about grandma?"

She paused. Then she said, "She is not part of your family anymore."

So that was it. I wouldn't be able to return to the home where I had been born just a few years before. Sometimes I would see Uncle Gicheol on the street. He would say hello and ask how I was doing. I was so sad. I couldn't play with him. I even missed those times that he would lecture me and force me to stand on one foot. If I had known this would happen, then I would have thrown even more pillows at him and made him promise to always discipline me, even if I didn't throw anything at him. I wished that I could have thrown a pillow at him, but I didn't even have a pillow. I had to use Mom's arm as a pillow.

I wondered to myself: "How can we not be a family anymore? We were having so much fun before, but not anymore. Does this happen to other families?" I passed by my old home every day on the way to preschool. Although my parents had gotten divorced, I saw my father very often. He was my father, but he wouldn't say anything to me, he wouldn't even say hello. He may have hated Mom, but I was his daughter. Couldn't he have hugged me at least once? Treated me the way a father treats a daughter? Couldn't he say, "I hate your mother, but you will always be my daughter"?

Instead, he was still so cold to me, treating me like I was a stranger. When I saw him on the street, I wanted to say: "Hi dad." But I couldn't. I would look at him, hoping he would reach out to me. When he saw me, he would look the other way or just walk past me without saying anything. One day, after Mom saw him and he didn't speak to her, she reminded me that he was not my father and that I should ignore him when I saw him.

In contrast, my grandma would cry and hug me when she saw me. "Did you eat? What did you eat?" My grandma was tall and skinny and pretty, then in her 50s. She was a tall woman, based on North Korean standards, about 5'4". She was always very kind. She was not the chatty type, and she didn't get into gossip about others.

Whereas my birth father had already removed me from his life, Mom and I had a bond that would grow deeper. After a few days, a neighbor brought us some rice.

It wasn't that much rice, but it was something special for us because we hadn't had rice in such a long time. Mom gave all of the rice to me, taking only vegetables for herself.

"Mom, let's eat together."

She said, "That's okay, I like vegetables."

"I'm not going to eat any rice if you don't eat some." I couldn't imagine eating rice while she ate vegetables. I felt so thankful for that neighbor bringing us even just a little rice. I felt more thankful to Mom for wanting to give me all the rice, and she was thankful that her daughter wanted to share it with her. Over the next few years, I would become even more grateful to have even just a few grains of rice.

MY PARENTS GOT DIVORCED in May of 1998. I will never forget my first birthday the September after that. It had been a tough time, mainly eating grass and vegetables leading up to my fifth birthday. There was no food to celebrate, we were barely surviving. Mom bought some white rice and cooked some meat. It had been a long time since I had seen white rice. "Today is your birthday," Mom said. "I don't have a gift for you, but today we can have white rice."

I was thrilled that we had white rice. I was staring at my bowl, but I couldn't eat. Mom had done it again; she had put almost all of the rice in my bowl. Mom's bowl had grass with a few sprinkles of rice.

I put down my spoon. "Mom, I'm not going to eat."

"Why? It's your birthday."

"Why are our bowls different?" I turned my head to

the side, ignoring the delicious white rice that I really wanted to eat. She insisted that I eat, but I couldn't. "I like white rice, but you only have grass. How can I eat?"

We were at a stand-off. She wanted to celebrate my birthday by having me eat white rice, and she was giving all of it to me. "Okay," she said. "How can I get you to eat the rice? It is hot, so eat it now."

I asked Mom to eat first. We went back and forth. "You first." "No, you first." "No, you first." We were interrupting each other, telling the other to eat first.

"Mom, let's eat it together. We can eat the rice first, then eat the grass after that." She agreed with that! Mom ate a little, then she said, "I'm full." I knew that she had not eaten much. It was my turn. I ate a little, it tasted so good, I could feel the rice dancing in my entire body. When I ate grass, I chewed for a long time, eating for the sake of survival. But white rice? I would quickly eat. It was so soft. I felt like I had gone back to a year before when I was always eating such delicious food.

"I'm full," I said, as I patted my stomach. We were two hungry people, mother and daughter, both pretending to be full so the other would eat. Mom looked at me. She was pleading with her eyes for me to obey her. "Really, it's okay for you to eat it. Why don't you go ahead and eat it today? It's your birthday."

"Because we don't eat rice very often," I said. "I want to eat it with you for my birthday. That is my real present." We began eating, taking turns eating a spoonful of rice. Mother, then daughter, then mother, then daughter. Finally, we got to the last spoonful of rice.

"Okay, this last one is for you," Mom said. I was happy and satisfied to have shared the meal with Mom. After resisting earlier, I opened my mouth wide, ready to be fed.

My mom fed me, laughing out loud. "You are like a little puppy."

We were both laughing, then I spread my arms wide in celebration, exclaiming, "Happy birthday to me!" We both laughed again. I remember thinking to myself, "I don't have a father, but I know I have a mom."

Mom and I lived in that barn for two years, as close as two people could be. It was terrible living in a barn, but I also loved it. I could see Mom every day. There wasn't an angry man there beating her. The barn was small and dirty, but it felt more peaceful than being at my father's home, which I no longer wanted to visit.

There wasn't enough food, but it was comfortable and peaceful. Mom was working in the daytime, then we would have dinner. Dinner time was two people laughing together, usually sharing boiled grass seasoned with salt.

The only thing I liked less than grass was radish. Springtime to summertime, we were usually eating grass. From the late fall to early winter, there was not much grass that was palatable. We were eating vegetables during that time, but I hated radish. When Mom was cooking, I would clean the barn or do homework. Then we would eat dinner together. I could smell radish as it was being cooked. Radish kimchi, radish side dishes, radish soup, everything radish. Even after eating it, which I didn't want to do, I would feel hungry again quickly.

Grass was still the main thing for us to eat during our time living in the barn. I tried to help Mom by going out to collect grass. Instead of being happy, Mom was angry. "You don't have to worry about eating," Mom said, probably trying to convince herself. "You should just worry about studying. I can worry about what we will eat."

"I'm sorry you are so busy, so I was trying to help. I knew that Mom was collecting wood after a busy day of work. I collected tree limbs to make it easier on her. I was too young to cut trees or to do anything physical.

Mom was surprised again. "How did you get so many tree limbs?" Her little baby seemed to be a good worker. But she wanted me to study, not out doing manual labor. "Don't ever do this again, you are too young to be out collecting grass or wood. I am your mom. The only thing you need to do is study."

I wanted to help Mom. I was young, but I knew we were struggling to survive. I would wake up at 7 a.m. every morning to get ready for preschool. She was farming rice and corn for the government, so she would leave at 8 a.m. and finish at 7 p.m. I looked forward to our time together in the morning and at night. I loved it when Mom would do my hair. Those moments were so precious to me. I knew she had long and difficult days working hard.

At 3 or 4 p.m., preschool would finish. Sometimes Mom would pick me up, at other times she would arrange for others to pick me up from preschool. One day it was raining hard. I was looking out the window, wondering when Mom would come. It was dark because of the clouds. Only one teacher was still there.

"Songmi-ya!" I heard a man's voice.

I was grumpy. It was a tall man who entered the room, a soldier. I didn't care about a soldier, I wanted to see Mom. The teacher called me. "Songmi-ya! This soldier says he will take you home."

"Why!?" I shouted. "He's not my mom! I'm scared! Mom should come pick me up." He was one of the soldiers who would run errands for Mom. Some of them knew us when we were wealthy, and they knew we had fallen on tough times. I didn't care that he was doing Mom a favor by picking me up, and he didn't care that I was complaining about him. He ignored me, then picked me up over his shoulder like I was a small bag of potatoes. The teacher was laughing as I fought to get away. The soldier ignored me and carried me away, delivering me to the barn.

After the soldier left, I was sitting in front of the door of the guard office, waiting for Mom. It was so boring; I had already finished my homework. I knew Mom was busy trying to make a good life for us. I thought: "What can I do to help Mom?"

She had told me to stop collecting grass, but I knew we needed more to eat. I left my school bag behind as I went to a warehouse nearby, carrying a hoe and a basket with me. I started collecting grass for us to eat. I didn't know how to collect grass, pulling as much soil as grass. I went home a little bit late. When I got back, Mom was frantic.

"Where were you? Where did you go?" She clearly had been worried. She had seen my bag, but not me. She had gone looking for me.

On the other hand, I was beaming with pride. "Mom, I finished my homework early. I didn't have anything to do, so I went to get grass for dinner."

She calmed down after I explained. "You are a kid," she said. "You are not an adult, you don't have to worry about food."

Her concerns didn't slow me down. "Here it is Mom," I said. There was as much soil as grass.

"Did you use the hoe?" she asked. "Next time, you should use a knife." She cleaned the grass, washed and boiled it, then she showed me how to collect grass. There are different kinds of grass. Some of it was more valuable, so we could sell it instead. We usually ate the less valuable grass. She showed me how to avoid damaging the grass when picking it.

I was so happy because I knew I was helping Mom. Dinner that night featured the grass that I had collected. It was so meaningful. The next day, I took the knife with me to properly gather grass. We were poor, and there was no food, but I was with Mom. It felt so comfortable. Even when she punished or lectured me, it was okay because I knew she loved me and wanted to teach me something. Also, I knew that Mom, despite her difficult life, never complained.

Mom would teach me things, review what I had learned in school that day, and sometimes we would sing together. It was not so easy for her to read to me because she was already tired from a hard day of manual labor. There were a few times as Mom read to me that my hair would get caught in the candle that was near us. Even that kind of thing was fine because we were together.

No matter how tough things were or how difficult they would get later, I could always look back on that special time of living in a barn with Mom.

3

LOSING HER VOICE AND SMILE

Songmi and her mom lived together in a barn for almost two years. If Songmi had died in that barn, then she would have died a happy child. It was a terrible situation, but she felt so loved by her mom. As mother and daughter struggled and suffered together, Songmi began to hate her father. He knew that they were living in a barn, but as far as she knew, he never did anything to help them.

Others were asking her mom, "Don't you want to get married again?" She told people she wasn't ready. Her focus was on taking care of Songmi. A neighbor said, "Your ex-husband has already restarted his life with another woman. When are you going to restart yours?" The neighbor didn't give up. "How long are you going to stay in a barn? You can marry a man with a house. You want to take care of Songmi, right? Every girl needs a mother and a father." It turned out that it wasn't just friendly advice. The neighbor had a specific man in mind. The neighbor drove the point home: "And Songmi won't be lonely when you are working, she can have sisters to play with."

Songmi's mom wanted to know about the family, but she was also being practical. She wanted a stable family situation. Most of all, she wanted a home. Songmi was six years old in the spring of 2000. Her mom told her about the conversation with the neighbor, then asked her, "Songmi-ya, what do you think? What if I get married again? You can have a father and two sisters. Also, we can leave this barn and live in a house again."

Her mother was happy and hopeful that they could have better lives. She was willing to marry another man so Songmi could have a more stable life. She went to meet the man and his daughters. Of course, they loved her. When Songmi's mom returned to the barn, they talked again. "I hope you are going to have a nice time with them," she said.

Songmi was excited. She would have two sisters! With this new family, she could be a baby sister and she could also have a baby sister to play with. "This is like a gift for me," Songmi said to herself. She had loved playing with Seolmi.

Once her mom decided, they began to move quickly. Songmi said goodbye to her preschool friends and got ready for her new life.

It was a sunny day, but that didn't matter. Even if it had rained, Songmi would have been dancing. It was going to be the start of a new life with a new family. When they first arrived there, they were all happy. Their two families had come together. Songmi couldn't stop smiling: "I have a father and sisters."

In his appearance, her stepfather couldn't compare to her birth father. Her stepfather was about 5'7" tall, so he was shorter than her father. He was skinny, unlike her father who was strong and fit. He wasn't handsome like her father. Looking at his appearance, Songmi couldn't see any way that he was better than her father. That wouldn't matter if he was kind. Her father was wealthy, but he didn't have a heart. She didn't know what the heart of this new father would be like.

The man who would become her new father said, "Hello, Songmi-ya, we will be living together. Let's be a happy family." She had never heard her father express joy and happiness. And her new father-to-be was saying her name in such a nice way.

Songmi was happy to meet her new sisters. They were eager to have a new mother. She later learned that their mother had died shortly after giving birth to the younger daughter. It was all joy at first. The older sister was named Eunkyung, her baby sister was named Seolkyung. To have the names sound similar, they gave Songmi the name Yukyung. It seemed that she would be part of the family. At first, when her mother called her "Yukyung-ah," Songmi was fine with it. They were going to be part of the family. But within a few days, Songmi could sense that something was wrong with her stepsisters.

IN OUR LIVES many people will come and go. Some teach us good things, and some teach us bad things; they can leave us with joy or scars in our hearts.

The worst person in Songmi's childhood was Eunkyung, the 10-year-old daughter in the new family. Her main problem? Songmi had a mother, and she didn't. The two new sisters were happy to have a new mother, but after their initial glee, they didn't welcome Songmi. They had a new mom, but they probably resented how close Songmi and her mother were. They had developed a tight bond while they were living together in the barn. Instead of understanding, the new sisters isolated Songmi. Eunkyung would glare at Songmi when she said "Mom." After a short time, Eunkyung started warning Songmi, "You can't call her by that name."

The sisters were a team united against Songmi. Eunkyung would say bad things about Songmi, and her shadow would repeat those things. It could have just been jealousy between young children struggling with the merger of two families, but Eunkyung's threats and warnings escalated.

When they were alone one day, Eunkyung threatened to beat Songmi, warning, "I will meet you in the street if you eat any side dishes." She wanted Songmi to eat only rice and soup, not delicious side dishes, such as kimchi or vegetables. On special occasions, such as national celebrations, it could be fish or meat, and Songmi knew she shouldn't eat that.

The next day, the family of five was sitting at the circular table with her stepfather and mom sitting together. Of course, Songmi wanted to sit next to her mom, but Eunkyung, as the oldest sister, would claim the seat next to her. Songmi would be sitting between the two sisters.

When Songmi lifted her chopsticks to eat from a side dish, Eunkyung pinched her under the table. Songmi dropped the food from her chopsticks when she saw Eunkyung glaring at her. One day, Songmi made a sound when Eunkyung pinched her. She wanted her parents to know what Eunkyung was doing. "Why did you pinch me?" Songmi asked, after making a loud "ouch" sound. Her mom and stepfather asked what was going on. "She pinched me because I wanted to eat a side dish," Songmi said, frustrated. "But not just today. She often pinches me when I try to eat something. Why can't I eat kimchi?"

Her mom asked Eunkyung what was going on. Looking at Songmi, Eunkyung said, "I was just teasing you."

After some back-and-forth, the parents were in agreement, "Don't do that again, we are family."

The reality was that they were becoming less like a family, however. Her mother and stepfather were arguing more often. Her stepfather was getting even lazier. Songmi's mom was working harder to sustain the family.

Songmi worried about letting the adults know what was going on. She didn't want to provoke the older and bigger girl. She told her mom, "I don't want to go to school."

The sentence didn't even register in her mother's mind: "You have to go to school. You have to study hard." She had always made sure that Songmi studied, even when they lived in the barn.

"I don't want to go."

"You have to go to school, you need to get a good education."

Songmi thought to explain, but they were in her stepfather's home. Her mother and stepfather were clashing more often, so Songmi had to be careful about causing trouble. As Songmi feared, Eunkyung was waiting down the street for her. "Shut up" is how she greeted Songmi. "You can't say anything." Her fist was balled up, ready to hit Songmi, but there were others around. When no one was around, she would threaten Songmi. When others were nearby, she would have a smile on her face as she pinched Songmi hard. She threatened to hurt Songmi if she screamed or let anyone know what was going on.

After that, Songmi spoke less at home, and when she did speak, she would look at Eunkyung first. After Songmi's "ouch," her mother was watching more closely. Then her mother divided the side dishes, so they each had their own food. Songmi was so happy. "Finally, I can have side dishes. I am not alone." She could see that her mom was on her side. They had to be careful about what they did in her stepfather's house, but her mother was still trying to send her a signal.

Songmi's stepsisters constantly told her, "She is not your mom." But she could see that when her mom was scooping rice for everyone, she would press the rice down so Songmi could have a little more. She would give it to Songmi last.

One day when Eunkyung noticed, she said, "Yukyung's bowl is heavy." She was jealous about everything. Songmi's mother dismissed the accusation, but she had to be careful about treating Songmi better than the others.

Although she feared being bullied by Eunkyung, Songmi was happy to be going to school again. A few days after the "ouch" incident, Songmi was at the door, dressed in her school uniform and with her backpack. "Mom! I'm going to school now."

"Wait a moment," her mom called out from the kitchen. She came to Songmi, and in one motion as she said goodbye, slipped something into Songmi's pocket, and told her, "Hurry up."

∾

WALKING DOWN THE STREET, Songmi could feel there was something warm in her pocket. She took it out and saw that it was some fried food. "Wow, Mom prepared some food just for me." She walked down the street, discreetly took a bite, then looked around to see if anyone was watching her. She took another bite. She was looking around for Eunkyung.

From that day, Songmi was always hopeful that she would get some fried food from her mom on the way to school. It didn't happen every day, but she was happy when she could feel the warm food that her mom had slipped into her pocket.

The two sisters were like mice, they would eat anything. One day, her mother had left food out that she would cook later. Eunkyung found the uncooked rice and started eating it. Her shadow did the same thing. The uncooked food looked so dirty, dusty, and moldy. It didn't matter — they ate it anyway.

Songmi was no longer the picky eater that she had been with her grandmother, but she still could not bring herself to eat some things. The sisters would eat anything and everything when her mom wasn't home. If there was some rice left out, uncooked, they would eat that too. Her mother was checking one day, confused about why there was less rice than she had expected. She even checked with the people who had sold her the rice to confirm the weight. That day, she asked them what had had happened to the uncooked rice.

Eunkyung jumped in: "Mom! Yukyung ate the rice." The liar was always ready to lie.

"What?" Her mother was incredulous. "How could you eat it uncooked?"

"Mom, I would never do that." It was Songmi's turn to

be incredulous, even a little outraged. She had started to lose her voice in the house, fearing to speak. In the two years they had lived in a barn together, sharing food, Songmi had refused to eat unless her mother ate. She didn't even steal food from neighbors, how could she steal food in her own house? Would her mother believe what the lying stepsister was saying?

Eunkyung may have been trying to break up Songmi's relationship with her mother, but her mom wasn't falling for it. "Yukyung-ah, I know you wouldn't do that."

Songmi felt relieved for the moment but still had an uneasy feeling. Eunkyung insisted, "Don't trust her, she is lying."

Songmi didn't say anything. She felt like nobody trusted her. And she knew Eunkyung might beat her later if she said anything or continued challenging her. Her mother couldn't always protect her.

She was young, but she could see that everyone in that family lied about anything and everything. It seemed like they preferred lying to telling the truth, and they could remember their lies better than most people could remember the truth. A person telling the truth can't change a story, but a good liar can say anything, adjust the lie to fit the moment, and sound more persuasive. They seemed to lie so they could practice getting better at lying.

The sisters next ate uncooked soybeans. Soybeans first need to be boiled and made into a square shape before being put outside. Those soybeans looked so pale after being put outside that Songmi couldn't believe that anyone would eat them.

One day, her mom wanted to make soybean sauce. They would first have to dry the *meju* (the main ingredient of soybean sauce). It was a sunny day, so she put the *meju* on the ground to dry. She then went out to sell soju in another area. Her mom had cooked lunch, but Songmi and her two stepsisters quickly ate everything. Songmi's stepsisters then began eating that smelly *meju*.

Eunkyung said, "Hey, you can try it, too."

"No way!" Songmi looked suspiciously at the *meju*.

"Don't be scared like a little girl, go ahead and try it."

The sisters seemed to enjoy eating it, so Songmi did get a little bit curious. She tasted it, and she was right, it didn't taste good, but it wasn't as bad as she had expected. Then all three of the young girls were sitting down, eating. After about 30 minutes, their stomachs were stuffed. The *meju* was dry, so they drank a lot of water to kill the thirst.

A bit later, Eunkyung thought about the time, realizing that Songmi's mom would be returning soon. They tried to rearrange everything, hoping she wouldn't notice. For once, the three girls were united as a team. Eunkyung asked Songmi, "Do you think it looks okay?" Songmi was hopeful but not confident.

They were sitting down, all watching the door, wondering when Songmi's mom would return. The door opened. "Mom," they all said in unison, all three kids looked at her.

The usual routine was that they would be playing, then the two sisters would go running to hug Mom. Songmi had become passive, withdrawn, speaking less often. She would trail them and sometimes not join at all. Their worst fears came true. The first thing Mom wanted to do was see how much the *meju* had dried.

She froze. Half of the *meju* was missing. "Did a mouse eat this much *meju*? Or did someone steal it? Were you three kids here all day? How could half of the *meju* be gone?" She was the only one talking, no one was answering her questions. Songmi realized that this time she had joined the sisters in their crime and might get blamed the most.

"You three kids, come here," she said. "Stand here."

The three kids stood in front of Mom, speechless. Usually, it was the two sisters united, but now all three were wondering what they needed to say. Seolkyung was in the center with Eunkyung and Songmi standing on either side of her. Eunkyung and Songmi looked at each other. Eunkyung was trying to give her a signal with her eyes. They were fidgeting. It would have been enough *meju* for them to eat as part of their side dishes for one year.

"What happened to your stomachs? Look at your stomachs! You cannot hide, you cannot lie. Your stomachs are telling me the truth!"

The *meju* had been dry when they ate it, but it expanded when it was mixed with liquid. They had drunk a lot of water after eating. Their swollen stomachs were evidence that they were the mice eating the *meju*. In frustration, Songmi's mom fell to her knees and sighed. "Is this real?"

Eunkyung would blame Songmi for eating or breaking things. In this case, clearly Songmi could not have eaten that much *meju* alone, and of course, their stomachs were swollen. Instead, Eunkyung claimed Songmi was the instigator: "Yukyung told us that we should eat it."

"So what happened to your stomach then?" Songmi's mom pointed at each of their bloated bellies. She stared at Songmi.

Songmi admitted what had happened. "Mom, it looked so dirty, I didn't want to eat it. They were saying to try it, so I tried it. At first, it tasted bad, then it got better, that's when we all ate."

All three kids were standing there with Songmi's mother looking them up and down. Songmi was scared. This time, she wasn't innocent. "No dinner for you kids. For one week, no lunch." She told Songmi's stepsisters to go to the other room. "Yukyung-ah, stay here."

When they were alone, her mom said, "You don't have to learn from them, they are teaching you bad things. When we first came to this home, you didn't follow them when they were eating uncooked rice and other things. Did I teach you bad things when we were living in the barn? For one week, you need to skip lunch." She explained that she was the only one supporting the family. "Look at your dad, he is just going out, but not making money. You three kids are at home, and you are doing this kind of thing. I'm losing energy."

"I'm so sorry, Mom." That was the last time that Songmi joined her stepsisters when they were causing trouble.

ONE DAY, Songmi was at home with the two sisters; her mom had gone out to sell things and her stepfather was out. Eunkyung began lecturing Songmi. "You need to obey me. Don't call me "sister," call me "Teacher."

Songmi said, "No, you're not a teacher. You're only three years older than me." Eunkyung suddenly began slapping Songmi.

"Follow me." Songmi followed her to the bedroom. Eunkyung locked the door, then began beating Songmi with a stick. Songmi was screaming, begging her to stop. A neighbor tried to open the door, but it was locked. She knocked on the door, saying, "Please open the door."

Eunkyung said, "This is not your business, leave us alone." The neighbor insisted, but Eunkyung ignored her. Turning to Songmi, she said, "You can't call her by the name 'Mom,' she is my mom. If you call her 'Mom' again, then I will beat you again, even worse than this. You need to obey me."

THE NEIGHBOR who had tried to stop Songmi from being beaten invited Songmi and her mom to her home. She asked Songmi's mom, "Do you know what happens to Songmi when you aren't here?"

Songmi remained quiet. She didn't want her mom to worry about her too much, knowing that her mom already had the burden of supporting the entire family. The neighbor explained what had happened. They looked at Songmi to explain.

"I don't obey her, so she beats me. She said that I need to call her 'Teacher.' She also said that I can't call you 'Mom.'"

"Teacher? Teacher of what? Stealing? Eating uncooked food?" Her mom was outraged.

The neighbor said, "Whenever you leave the house, you should take your daughter with you. Otherwise, she may get beaten and I can't do anything about it." But her mom couldn't take only Songmi.

Her mother and stepfather had been having more trouble. Her mother had already gotten divorced once and wasn't sure if this new man was right for her. As their disagreements and then arguments started to escalate, her stepfather was concerned that Mom might run away with Songmi. She wanted to take Songmi with her when she went out to sell things, but he would always object.

The next day, she asked all three kids, "Who wants to follow me? If you want to, then put your hand up." Songmi had been a talkative and active tomboy just a few years before, but her lack of confidence and low self-esteem paralyzed her at that moment. She had stopped talking, only answering when she was spoken to, and was afraid that she would say or do the wrong thing. Songmi couldn't speak, couldn't complain, and at this moment, she couldn't move when she most needed to do so. Eunkyung did so immediately, enthusiastically raising her hand. Her shadow did the same thing.

"Okay," her mom said, speaking with less enthusiasm. "Let's go." Then Songmi finally got the courage to say, "I want to go with you too."

Her stepfather said, "You can't go with her, you must stay home."

Songmi was the hostage to make sure her mother returned. Songmi started crying. She feared her stepfather; she didn't want to be alone with him.

"Mom, please take me too," Songmi said.

Her mother said, "No, your dad told you to stay."

It was true that Songmi had a mom, but her stepsisters had a father, and they were in his home. Songmi started crying again, then her mom whipped her.

It was getting dark; her mom had left with her stepsisters. Songmi was sitting outside the door, crying. Her stepfather was inside smoking. Her birth father had never comforted her and now this new stepfather turned out to be no better. Her stepfather was never on her side. If the sisters were arguing or fighting, then her stepfather would tell her, "You need to listen to what Eunkyung says." Even if he didn't know what was going on, her stepfather would blame Songmi. Her mom was more like a judge. She would listen to everyone, then admonish whoever was the troublemaker.

Songmi had hesitated earlier when her mother had asked who had wanted to go with her, but now, Songmi thought about her situation. Suddenly, she stood up. She ran. Both her mother and stepfather had told her to stay. She had been taught to always respect and obey them, but suddenly she was running.

She was going to find her mom. She was running, but it was already dark, and she was scared. A woman had recently been killed on that road, and the killer was still on the loose. Up the road, Songmi could see three people walking ahead, one adult and two children. As she got closer, she could hear the soothing sound of her mom's voice. Songmi was trying to be quiet as she followed them, trying to stay out of sight.

"Is someone there?" Her mom looked around. Turning her attention to the two sisters, she said, "Hey girls, let's take a break." They were sitting about 30 meters from Songmi. She could hear their voices. They sat for about 10 minutes. Songmi wasn't sure if she should approach them.

"Does Mom know that I am following her?"

Her mother and stepsisters arrived at another area to sell soju. Songmi had continued following them, still hiding herself. It was already late so the people they were meeting said they could sleep there. She heard her mom say, "There are four of us, another daughter is coming."

Songmi was looking down, but then she looked up, sideways with a happy smile. She no longer had to hide. She stepped forward so everyone could see her.

"Mom, she's here," Eunkyung said. "How could she run away from Dad? You both told her to stay home. That's not good!"

"Yes, that's right, she's here, so let's have a good time," her mom said.

4

MOM LEFT

A fter having such a loving two years as mother and daughter sharing a small barn, the time in her stepfather's home had been like hell. Sometimes when Songmi and her mom were alone, they could talk as mother and daughter. "Mom," Songmi finally said one day. "I miss the barn. Can we go back? Living in a barn with you was better than living here. Even the hut was better."

Her mom was stunned the first time Songmi asked. "No. We can't go back. I also regret that we came here. I didn't know they would be like this." After six months, the whole family was on the verge of collapsing. Her mother pleaded with Songmi's stepfather, "We need to survive. We need to work together." She was working hard to sell things, but he was contributing less and less. He was like a lazy teenage boy who didn't take responsibility. He had no morality, ethics, or standards for himself or his daughters. Songmi's mom would lecture and discipline her in front of the others to make sure Songmi didn't pick up their bad habits.

Her lazy stepfather had reached a new level of laziness. He would lounge around the home, often plucking his facial hair. Finally, he decided he didn't want to go out anymore to collect wood. Instead, Songmi's mother would buy it with money she had made. Later, she was the one collecting wood and cooking things to sell. Finally, they had their biggest argument that ended everything.

A neighbor in a wheelchair had come to the home when Songmi's mom was out. "Where's my dog?" He said it smelled like the family had killed an animal and eaten it. He pointed at Eunkyung. "Do know what happened to my dog?"

Songmi's lying stepsister did what she does best: she lied without hesitating. Eunkyung told the neighbor, "I didn't steal your dog. My mom stole the dog." Songmi's stepfather also blamed Songmi's mom.

The neighbor was skeptical. "This family has been known for being thieves before the new woman showed up." He was in no position to challenge Songmi's stepfather physically, so he turned around in his wheelchair and left. His family was also in a difficult situation. His daughter was in the hospital with a serious medical condition.

Songmi's mom got angry when she learned what had happened. She had never joined in their stealing. They would steal chickens, rabbits, dogs and wood. They were so lazy, they preferred to steal instead of working hard. They would even steal dog poop from other people. Stealing dog poop wasn't enough, Eunkyung stole the entire dog. Stealing food was understandable, but it was not acceptable to kill and eat someone else's pet.

When Songmi came home from school that day, she could feel that something had happened. She opened the door and saw that only her stepfather was there. He was on his back, looking at a mirror, plucking his facial hair.

"Where's Mom?" He didn't answer immediately. Then he spoke in a serious voice, "Your mom left." He paused. "She said she will come back. She is going to your grand-mother's house."

A chill went through Songmi's entire body. This was the second time she had left Songmi suddenly. The first time had been when Songmi was four years old, but there was still some security in her life with Grandma Bae. But with this family, she was an outsider. They had wanted her mom as their mother and wife. They had accepted Songmi as part of the package.

"When is she coming back?" Songmi couldn't hide her panicky feeling.

"She said she will come back in a week." His voice was flat.

Songmi didn't respond. She asked herself, "How can I live for one week without Mom?" Songmi worried about what would happen to her with this family. She was afraid to be alone with her stepfather. She asked where her step-sisters were.

"They are playing near the river."

"Can I go play with them?"

"No," he said. "Get dinner ready." His voice was icier than before. The tone in his voice let Songmi know that her life was about to get more difficult. "Peel the potatoes," he said, "and get some grass." She walked outside. Songmi could see that her stepsisters were playing in the water. "Sisters, let's get some grass for dinner."

"No," Eunkyung said. "Father said we can play." Songmi peeled the potatoes, washed the grass, and got ready for dinner. Later, Eunkyung came in from playing to cook. Songmi, in a daze, helped her as required. She wished that her mom would come back sooner than one week. A few days later, a neighbor told Songmi, "Your mom said she is going to come back to get you."

Initially it had felt like a gift that they were joining the family, but now Songmi was left on her own, at the mercy of her stepfather and stepsisters. Songmi was only six or seven years old, trying to figure out how to get out of the house. After her mom left, Songmi stopped talking. She had already become passive, speaking only when spoken to and said just enough to avoid trouble. Now, her voice was gone. She was sleepwalking through every day as she waited for her mom to return.

After her mother left, her stepfather talked with even more anger in his voice. He had said Songmi's mother would be back after a week, but weeks went by. With each day, her stepfather was getting more frustrated with Songmi. She felt so insecure at that point, unsure what would happen to her. He often yelled at Songmi about small things. They were both waiting for her mom.

"Hey, wake up." Her stepfather was lazy, but he was diligent about waking up Songmi every morning at 6 a.m. "Go get me 50 cigarettes." Songmi would walk to the Inheung train station looking around for discarded ciga-rettes. There were many people at the train station, so there were many cigarette butts to pick up. Her stepfather wanted them all, no matter how small the cigarettes were. He would roll them together in a newspaper to make a longer cigarette. There were many cigarettes, but also a lot of competition, especially with homeless people, to get them.

It was more difficult for Songmi when she went with Eunkyung. Her stepsister would claim the first batch of

cigarettes. Then Songmi had to scramble to pick up cigarettes so her stepfather wouldn't yell at her. They would
even search the garbage dump for cigarette butts. They
often had a second reason to visit the garbage dump: to
find something to eat. At home, her stepsisters were like
mice eating anything. Songmi had stooped to their level.
When she was three years old, she had been such a picky
eater. But three years later, she was looking for food in
garbage dumps. Even if there was a wrapper, she would
lick it if there had been some food inside it at some point.

Someone had thrown away a crab. It was so dirty, and
the crab had already dried up. There was very little left,
but Songmi was chewing and eating it like it was freshly
cooked. "Uhm, yummy," she said to herself. They had to
be quicker than desperate homeless people when it came
to grabbing cigarette butts, and they had to be even faster
in eating discarded food. The adults would sometimes yell
for them to get away. They would run when they heard,
"Hey! Get out of here!" When Songmi was by herself, she
would run as soon as she heard "Hey!"

Her stepfather would send her out with Eunkyung to
pick up dog poop he could use as fertilizer. If they saw a
dog, they would look around to see if there was any dog
poop for them to pick up. He might order them to each
pick up at least 30 pieces of dog poop. Like with cigarette
butts, Songmi always had to let Eunkyung get them first.

They would feel like they had hit the jackpot when
they saw human poop. It was better fertilizer than dog
poop, so her stepfather would be more pleased. Every
morning when she opened her eyes, Songmi knew her to-
do list: to collect cigarette butts and dog poop. She was six
or seven years old, but one thing that was not on her to-do
list: going to school.

Sometimes Songmi's school mates would visit her stepfather's home to ask her to join them. They would ask her stepfather why Songmi couldn't go to school. He told them they didn't have food or wood to give to the school. The first time, there were two people who visited to invite her to return to school. With each visit there seemed to be more people. On one visit, there were about 12 people. Songmi was so embarrassed because everything about them was poor. Finally, her stepfather relented.

Songmi went to school for a few days, but it was less fun than preschool, for a few main reasons. One, their increasingly chaotic family situation was weighing on Songmi's mind. It was getting to be more difficult for her to smile. Her stepfather was getting meaner and talking more roughly to Songmi, she was isolated from the rest of her stepfather's family, and her mom still hadn't returned. Two, her "small potato." She didn't have any nice clothes and her shoes had holes in them. Other children would laugh and say, "I see your small potato." That is, they could see her toes. Three, Songmi usually didn't have food for lunch. Songmi's classmates would have something to eat, but she didn't have anything at all.

At age seven, anyone who had seen her would have wondered if she was having psychological problems or they might have correctly guessed that she was in a troubled family. A few years before, she had been a playful child who laughed at everything. At seven years old, she didn't smile. She didn't talk in school or the house. She didn't say anything. When others played and laughed, she would look at them and wonder, "Why are they so happy? How can I be happy like them?"

Songmi was thinking about running away, but she had no idea where to go. Her stepfather seemed to be watching her, constantly checking on her whereabouts. Going back to school got Songmi thinking about looking for her mom. Being back in school gave her an unexpected feeling of freedom. When she was out collecting cigarettes or dog poop, she didn't feel free. She knew that her stepfather would be expecting her to return quickly to bring him back things. On the other hand, he would be expecting her to be at school most of the day.

That morning, Songmi woke up thinking about going to look for her mom. At lunchtime, Songmi left as usual while the others ate. She stood in front of the school door, checking the time. She started walking, but not in the direction of her stepfather's home. Instead, she asked others which direction was Shinsang-gu. Perhaps her mother was at Grandma Choi's home. Songmi could escape her stepfather's family and be at a place where her mother could still find her one day. It was about 12:30 p.m. Her stepfather might not start to wonder about her until about 5 p.m.

"Okay," she told herself. "Let's go find Mom." She didn't want to go back to her stepfather, there was nothing at his home for her. When she asked people how she could get to Shinsang-gu, they would be surprised a little girl was trying to walk such a very long distance.

"Little girl, you're too young to be walking there on your own. Where are your parents?" She didn't explain that she didn't have a father, that she wanted to get away from her terrible stepfather and his terrible family, and that she was looking for her mom. She would tell them that she was going to them.

She knew it would take a long time, so she started running. When she got thirsty, she went to the river to drink water out of it, like a dog. It was the hot summertime. She would occasionally see people, always wishing one of the women was her mom. She saw a woman who looked somewhat like her mom, but she was a long distance away. The woman had long hair and was fashionably dressed. Songmi was tired, she had no energy, her shoulders drooped as she walked.

When the woman got closer, Songmi realized that it was her mom! Her mom recognized her. They had both been walking, but suddenly they were running to each other. After months of being isolated, she was finally with her mom. She couldn't believe her good luck; this was truly a gift for her. She was looking for her mom who just happened to be coming to get her that day. They were hugging each other. After such a terrible time in her stepfather's home, she finally felt like a daughter again.

Her mom asked her many questions. Songmi said she didn't have a chance to leave the house before today, but her stepfather finally let her go to school, so she had a chance to get away. "That's why I was looking for you."

"How in the world were you going to find me?" Songmi told her that she only knew the city name, but not the address of Grandma Choi's home. "How did you think you could find me?"

"I didn't know," Songmi said. "I needed to leave that house to try to find you." It was a long walk to Grandma Choi's home, but Songmi was happy to be with her mother. She had stayed at her stepfather's home for a year. She had become passive, quiet, and rarely spoke. Songmi had lost her smile and her voice in that home. She was happy to be finished with that family.

5

LOOKING FOR MOM

*S*ongmi *got out of bed to use the toilet. The bedroom was on the right side, the outhouse was on the left. She opened the door to the bedroom, walked between the two dressers where there was a small space between them. There, she hunched down to pee. Everything looked fuzzy to her.*

She looked straight ahead, saw her mother seated on the floor. Her mom's face was pale, her eyes closed. Songmi's eyes focused — her mom was dead. Songmi started screaming.

"What's wrong with you? Why are you screaming?" It was the voice of Ms. Kim, the neighbor that Songmi was living with. Songmi's mom had left her with Ms. Kim while she went to make money elsewhere. Songmi had been waiting patiently for a few weeks, then she was sleepwalking through the days and weeks. That nightmare woke up Songmi, both literally and figuratively.

"I want to see Mom. I want to see her face." Songmi told Ms. Kim about the nightmare, that she wanted to see that her mom was alive.

She started asking around and heard that her mother

had gone to a different area but had lost everything and couldn't return. She was probably staying at a friend's home.

""That is a long way," Ms. Kim said. "You have no idea how far it is, and you don't know how to get there." She could see that Songmi had already made up her mind. "Okay, I cannot stop you. Please, be careful. Be sure to ask people about for directions so you don't get lost." Ms. Kim was expressing concern for Songmi, but then she made the mistake of mildly criticizing her mother. Songmi had heard people criticize her mother before, and she had overwhelming responses even to adults. Ms. Kim asked, "Why is your mom making you look for her?"

Songmi said, "Don't say that! You don't know Mom and her situation; she is trying very hard." Songmi could never forget how hard her mother had worked to support the stepfather's family. "I only have one Mom in my life."

Ms. Kim apologized to Songmi. She said that her mom had not abandoned her as many parents had been doing. There were many street kids who were homeless. Her mom did always seem to find a place for Songmi to stay as she tried to make money.

SONGMI WAS RUNNING. She had walked at first to look for her mom but couldn't wait and started running so she could find her mother sooner. But what if she wasn't at her friend's home? Where would Songmi look next? She got tired, started walking again, and started singing to herself. The songs were about mothers. She had learned the songs from friends, not from school. Then Songmi got thirsty. Whenever she saw someone selling water, she would ask, "Can I drink some water? I'm thirsty, but I don't have any money."

One woman gave her a drink. That water tasted so good at that moment. Songmi was grateful. She asked so many people for directions. Sometimes she would come to a fork in the road and would just wait for an adult to come by so she could ask them for directions.

"Excuse me," Songmi would say to a passerby, "I want to go to Inheung. Which way should I go?"

She would always see concern in the eyes of people as they tried give her directions. She was a child in raggedy clothing, she wasn't carrying anything, she was alone, and walking a long distance. Sometimes Songmi would come to another fork in the road with two or three different paths. As she got closer, Songmi asked many people about the house she was trying to find. Finally, she arrived. She had left her neighbor's house early that morning, then walked, ran, and sang for 12 hours, hopeful that she could find Mom. She hadn't eaten once.

She knocked on the door, and her mom's friend opened it. "Oh my, Songmi is here!"

"Really?" It was her mom's voice from the other room.

In Songmi's nightmare a week earlier, she had been dead. But here she was alive, coming to her. Songmi was grabbing her, checking her body, touching her face, checking that everything was okay.

"What's wrong with you?" her mom asked. Songmi gave her a big hug as she cried.

"Mom, I had a nightmare. You were dead."

As Songmi explained, her mother had a serious look on her face. "Oh, my goodness. You were having a nightmare the same night I tried to kill myself."

She explained that she had taken poison on her

birthday, on May 20th. It was the first time she spoke directly to Songmi about her difficulties with making money, how she felt terrible that she hadn't been able to provide more for Songmi, and that she often had to be away from her as she tried to make money. She had left Songmi to shield her from these problems and kept it all inside. Her mother was probably suffering psychologically from the death of her daughter, from being blamed consistently by her former husband about it, the beatings that she had suffered at the hands and feet of her first husband, the stress of her second failed marriage, and her shame at her inability to take care of Songmi on her own. Depressed and drinking, she decided to end her life.

Songmi wasn't completely shocked. Suicide is something that she had also thought about. She was sad to hear that her mother was also thinking about it. It made her more determined not to be in her mother's way.

Songmi's mother said that when she didn't die, she regretted what she had done. She thought about Songmi. She didn't tell Songmi at the time, but she had felt that she had failed as a mother. She would try even harder to make money so she could properly take care of Songmi one day.

THEY HAD dinner that night with some food her mom had bought even though she didn't have much money.

"Mom, don't spend too much money."

"No, you're my daughter," she said. "I want to treat you to a good meal." Such meals were rare those days. They had some meat and vegetables that her mom's friend cooked. Songmi updated them about her life with Ms. Kim.

Addressing them all, Songmi said, "She told me to wait for Mom, but I couldn't wait, especially after I had the nightmare."

Songmi felt so good that she had found her mom, but then reality hit.

Her mom said, "Okay, tomorrow you need to go back to Ms. Kim's house."

Songmi was so disappointed. She looked down at the floor, unable to meet her mother's eyes. She lifted her head, her hair covering half her face. She looked at her at last.

"When can I see you again, Mom?"

She told Songmi that she had lost the money that she had borrowed from someone. She made it clear that she was doing her best to make money so they could be together.

"I will make money soon, then I will go to you after that. My baby, please wait for me. I am trying hard to give you a good life, but it is very tough now."

The next morning, after breakfast and many tears, Songmi said goodbye. Her mother gave her a little money so Songmi could buy something to eat or drink along the way.

Songmi made the long trip back to Ms. Kim's house, getting lost many times along the way. But even when she knew the way, Songmi would ask others. Sometimes she just wanted to talk to people. There's a Korean proverb, "Even when you know the way, you need to ask others."

Sometimes Songmi would be looking at the clouds, hoping the Sun would come out again soon. "Maybe the Sun went to eat lunch?" That's what she would ask her mother when they were together. "Maybe the Sun went to the toilet? Or maybe the Sun is sleepy?" And sometimes, she would talk directly to the Sun. "Hi, Sun. Did you have lunch? Are you tired?"

Songmi would guess the time based on her shadow. Her mom had taught her how to tell the time without a clock. Whenever Songmi was looking for her mom, she would look at her shadow and talk to the Sun.

"YOU'RE HERE! Did you see your mom?" Ms. Kim welcomed Songmi back.

"Yes! But she can't come back now because she lost money."

Then Ms. Kim again made the mistake of criticizing her mom. As always, Songmi was quick to respond. "Hey!" Songmi said. "Don't say bad things about Mom."

Ms. Kim said, "Okay, okay." She had learned that whenever Songmi heard people say bad things about her mom, she would glare at or even argue with them. Songmi was a child who had been taught to respect those older than herself, but she made an exception whenever anyone said anything bad about her mom.

One time when Songmi was peeling potatoes, she heard two neighbors talking about her mother. They were saying that parents must take care of their kids.

Songmi stopped peeling and turned in their direction to face them. "I can hear what you are saying! How can you talk like that? Don't you know her daughter is here?"

"You look so pitiful, we are worried about you," one of the neighbors said. "You always smile, but it seems that you are hiding your true feelings."

"You don't have to worry about me, I didn't ask you for anything. No one can be sure about anyone else's life, we all have different situations," Songmi retorted. "I have my life, you have yours." Songmi said it with pride but she also knew her reality. Songmi had lost her smile at her stepfather's home, but she had begun smiling again. But she wondered to herself about her smile.

Songmi continued waiting at Ms. Kim's home, but she was getting restless. She told Ms. Kim that she was going to look for her mom and wasn't sure that she would be back. Songmi knew that Ms. Kim was frustrated because her mother hadn't paid Ms. Kim lately for taking care of Songmi. Songmi had no idea where she could go, but there was one place: Grandma Bae's home. It took her about 10 hours to walk there.

Songmi's stepmother had told her, "Never come back." At that moment, Songmi didn't care. She was looking for her mother. She knocked on the door, but at first no one answered. She was trying to peek inside. She could see that it looked the same with animals walking around. The dog was panting.

Her grandmother asked, "Who's there?"

"Grandma!" she answered, "It's Songmi!"

Grandma Bae came running. "Oh my! Is it really you?" She welcomed her inside. She was preparing dinner, but she gave Songmi something to eat immediately. Her father arrived a few minutes later. He hadn't seen his daughter in more than a year. He hadn't changed.

"Why are you here?"

"I'm looking for Mom."

"Where are you staying now?"

She explained that she was staying at a neighbor's house, but that Mom hadn't paid her. Her stepmother didn't look happy to see her. The last time she had seen her she had said, "Never come back." This time, Songmi's stepmother said, "Oh, you're here again."

Songmi remained silent. Grandma Bae interjected, "She's looking for her mom."

Her stepmother asked, "Why is she looking for her mom in this house?" Songmi looked down at the floor. She didn't have an answer. She didn't know how to explain everything they had been through. She had been overjoyed to see her grandmother, and even felt warm being back in her first home, but her father and step-mother brought her back to reality.

Grandma Bae said, "That's enough. Let's not ask her too much."

Her grandmother asked if Songmi would like to see her two sisters, but her stepmother said, "They are not her sisters."

Grandma Bae said, "Don't say that. She can under-stand everything, so please be careful of what you are saying."

Songmi had already heard that her father had two children with her stepmother, but she didn't feel like they were her sisters. She loved babies, but in this case, she didn't feel the urge to play with them.

Her stepmother was still grumbling, but Grandma Bae took charge. Clearly, something was different this time. Grandma Bae may have taken charge because it was an emergency. She asked Songmi's father and uncle to deliver about 15 pounds of dry corn to Ms. Kim.

"Okay, let's go there," her father said. Songmi rode behind her father on the bicycle. For the first time in a while, Songmi was with her father. She should have grabbed him around his waist, as most daughters would have done. But Songmi held onto the bicycle seat instead of holding onto him. He didn't say anything. He was running an errand. Her father and uncle didn't go inside Ms. Kim's home. Her uncle said, "Please care for her."

Ms. Kim was happy to receive the dry corn, but Songmi felt like she couldn't remain there. She didn't know if her mom would be able to pay Ms. Kim next month, and she couldn't expect Grandma Bae's help again. Songmi told Ms. Kim, "I will try to find Mom."

Songmi went to Grandma Choi's house at Shinsang-gu. She felt so lonely, even though she was with several family members. Songmi felt like she was by herself. No one was taking care of her, she didn't have anyone she could talk to about things, no one she could complain to about her life. Songmi really missed Grandma Bae and Uncle Gicheol.

After a few months of waiting and feeling unloved at Grandma Choi's home, Songmi asked herself: "Would they really miss me if I left?" When Songmi bumped into people who had worked with her mom, she would ask, "Have you seen my mom?"

One woman said, "Yes, I saw your mom. She's homeless at Geumya Station."

Songmi couldn't believe what she was hearing. "Oh no. How could that be? Mom said that she would make money to come back home."

The woman told Songmi, "Your mom is trying to make money. You can wait, she will come to you."

Songmi hadn't believed the woman who said her mom was homeless, but the things she had heard made it seem possible. Aunt Yeonhui had said a few times that Songmi's mom might die on the street. There had been many such cases of people freezing or starving to death.

"Maybe Mom really is homeless?" Once Songmi began to accept that her mom really might be homeless, she thought: "If Mom is homeless, I can be homeless with her. How could I be staying in a home while Mom is homeless at a train station?"

She waited a few days, then said to herself, "I'm going to find Mom." She was too young to take the train by herself, but she could walk. Songmi didn't know where she should go. "See," Songmi told herself. "You don't have to tell them. They don't really care. You can just leave."

Songmi walked out the door. She only had the clothes she was wearing and her voice to ask for directions.

"Excuse me. How can I get to Geumya Station?"

"Hey sweetie, that's too far. Do you know where your mom is?"

"Yes, I know, she is at Geumya Station! That's why I want to go there."

She arrived at the station at dinner time, tired and hungry.

"Excuse me, have you seen a beautiful lady? I'm looking for my mom. She has big eyes, long hair, she's not that tall. She's a little bit fat. Have you seen her?"

She couldn't find her mom at Geumya Station. Next, she went back to Inheung, where she had previously found her mom after her nightmare. But she wasn't there either. Songmi hit the road again, looking for her mother. She sat down for a few minutes to rest, then fell asleep. Songmi woke up in a different place. She was on a bed of rice straw. She didn't have a pillow or a blanket. Looking around, there were no windows, the walls were crumbling, and there was a hole in the ceiling. It was an old warehouse.

It was early January. Songmi opened the door, ready to leave this unknown place. At that moment, an elderly woman was coming in. "You woke up!"

"Yes. May I ask who you are?" Whispering, struggling to get the words out, dizzy from exhaustion, Songmi was losing her battle with hunger.

The woman told her that she would be back in a minute. Inside the house next to the warehouse, the woman argued with her son. He asked, "How can you bring in another homeless person? We are also poor. What can we give to them?"

She said, "You can't say that. We need to share what we have. Even kimchi, salt or water."

She came back to Songmi in the warehouse. "Please drink this." She handed Songmi some kimchi soup. "Don't ever sleep outside, especially in such cold weather. I have seen many people freeze to death outside. If I hadn't found you, you could have died. I'm so sorry, I wish you could stay here longer, but it's not easy. We are also poor. My son is so angry now."

Songmi left the warehouse. She had new energy after having a little kimchi soup. Songmi resumed searching for her mother.

AFTER TWO MONTHS back at Grandma Choi's home, Songmi went looking for her mom again at Geumya Station. Songmi went a different way, looking for a short-cut. Songmi saw two soldiers coming from the opposite direction. The soldiers did a double-take when they saw her. Was that really a little girl out walking by herself late at night?

"Little one, where are you going?"

"To Bongsan-ri."

"Hey kid, it's too late out, we can't let you go by yourself. Come to our military unit. Have you had dinner?" Songmi shook her head no. He said, "My goodness, come with us."

They took her to a home near the military base. The platoon leader checked Songmi's backpack. Her aunt had given her lunch. It was the ingredients used to make a North Korean dish that is similar to tofu. The food was for animals. It was something that North Koreans were eating for survival.

"How can you eat this? How can they feed you this? You can sleep here tonight," the platoon leader said. "Then tomorrow we can help you try to find your mom."

The next day, they took her to her father's home. Grandma Bae welcomed her, was happy to feed her, but added: "You have to leave quickly."

The platoon leader asked, "Why? Why should she leave quickly?"

Her grandmother explained that Songmi's stepmother might be angry. Songmi had come looking for her mother before, and her grandmother had taken a stand. This time, she was more reluctant. It was possible after Songmi left last time that her stepmother had made it clear that she really didn't want Songmi there. After some more small talk, Grandma Bae said, "Your stepmother is coming soon."

The platoon leader was frustrated by the conversation. He picked Songmi up, put her on his back, and started walking. Songmi punched his shoulders, pinched his ears, and even tried to tickle him. "Let me down!" He was trained to fight grown men, especially American soldiers, so of course Songmi was no challenge for him. Songmi wanted to see her mom, but that wouldn't be possible if he took her back to the military unit.

"I know you miss your mom; she will find you," the platoon leader said. "You are in danger when you are out walking around by yourself. You are too young, and a girl. If your mother told you to stay somewhere, then stay there and wait for her."

Songmi told him about her family's situation. The soldier got emotional as he listened; he wanted to support Songmi. What did she want to do while she stayed with his military unit?

"I can read, but I don't know how to write." He bought her nice clothes including Adidas sportswear, shoes, pencils, books, and gave Songmi some money so she could buy some food. He was from a rich family in Pyongyang. He became like the big brother she never had and was the first positive male influence in her life. He said he would later like to bring her to live with him as his younger sister. That sounded exciting to Songmi because she had never been to Pyongyang.

He wanted to take Songmi to her aunt's home to wait for her mom, but Songmi said no. She wanted to find her mom. When it was time for Songmi to go, he started crying. Songmi didn't remember ever seeing her father or stepfather cry, so it shocked her that a man was concerned about her.

"I'm really worried about you," he said. "I hope you can find your mom. Please don't forget about me and don't forget to call me." He gave Songmi his phone number and address.

It was a sad goodbye for Songmi. She started walking again to Geumya Station, looking for her mom. She fell asleep on a bench. When Songmi woke up, the nice clothes, shoes, money, backpack, everything that the platoon leader had given her was gone. They had even stolen the paper with the soldier's phone number and address on it.

6

HOMELESS

Songmi spent months walking around looking for her mom. Could she believe her eyes? Her mom was running in her direction. Songmi had asked homeless people at Geumya Station if they had seen her mother. One homeless woman said, "Yes, I have seen her! She's here."

"I'm her daughter," Songmi said. The woman said she would be back, then a few minutes later Songmi saw her mom running to her. They were both crying and hugging each other.

"Why didn't you come back? I was waiting for you every day."

Her mom said, "I can't go back until I make money to repay my debt."

Songmi and her mother were homeless and starving at Geumya Station. A homeless boy named Hyuk came running to Songmi and her mom. "Come on, let's go! This is a rich train!" When Songmi didn't move, Hyuk asked, "What are you doing? You're not going to the train?"

"Why are you going there?" Songmi didn't know what they were supposed to do.

Hyuk said, "Hey, come on! You don't know how to get food from people on the train? Come on! It's easy, I will show you how!" Trains coming from or going to Pyongyang or near the border to China would mean there were rich people on the train.

Dizzy from hunger, Songmi slowly followed him. "You don't look homeless," he said. "You need to look poor." Songmi had been homeless for only a few days and was still tidy. Hyuk said, "You need to make your face look dirty, put some dirt on it."

"No!" Songmi said, "I can't do that."

"What?" Hyuk said. "Whatever! Just come with me." He pointed to three people who were sitting down and eating. "You see that? They have a lot of food, right? Watch, I will go first." He walked over to them. "Please, give me a little food."

"Hey kid! Get out of here, you look dirty."

Hyuk tried another group. Songmi didn't say anything. Her eyes were glued to the food. One man said, "Hey, little one. Are you hungry?" She nodded her head without speaking. "Okay, come here, sit down here."

She didn't eat even though they had given her food. They asked her why she wasn't eating. Songmi asked, "Can I take this food to my mom? She's starving, she can't even move now."

They got visibly emotional. "You're so small and worried about your mom. Wait here." They then went to get more food from the train. They came back and said, "This is for our trip, but please share it with your mom." They wished her luck. "We hope you won't be homeless for long."

"You saved me and my mom." Songmi thanked them several times, then she rushed to her mom. "Mom! Here's some rice." Her mom slowly turned her head to face Songmi, then smiled.

A few minutes later, Hyuk came back to them. "Wow! How did you get such great food?"

Songmi explained that the three people had given her food. Hyuk rushed to get some side dishes. The three of them together. After having a great meal, they went back to get more food. She saw the same three people there. They suggested to Songmi that she could go to the kitchen room on the train and ask for food. But they told her she should go alone. If many homeless went together then they would be less likely to receive any food. Songmi walked to the train, looking at the kitchen car. She didn't say anything, she just looked.

One woman was looking outside. "Hey little one!" she said. She held a bucket. Many homeless kids watching her started walking and running in her direction. The woman was clear. She said, "No no no, not you." Some of the bigger kids were also coming, but the woman said, "No, not you." Then she pointed at Songmi. "You, little girl. Come here." She gave Songmi a bucket. "Can you bring some water? Then I can give you food."

Songmi returned with a bucket of water. The woman gave her a lot of food. "Little one, can you hold it all?"

"I can do it!" Songmi had new energy. Songmi went back to her mom. "The kitchen woman on the train gave it to me," Songmi said, beaming.

Hyuk was amazed, "Wow, today is your lucky day."

During the winter there were fewer lucky days. Some of the homeless people that Songmi knew starved or froze to death. Songmi's mother often left her with relatives or neighbors as she tried to make money, but she had not abandoned her as many of the children at the train station had been deserted by their parents.

Songmi noticed that one kid who was usually with a group of homeless kids had been missing for about a week. Songmi asked Hyuk about the kid. "Oh, you don't know?" Hyuk asked. "He's dead." Songmi was shocked. He was so young; how could he be dead? He usually slept near the market area of the train station. If the trains didn't stop, then he could beg for food from people selling things in the market.

"What did they do with his body?" Songmi was trying to understand. Hyuk said, "Somebody probably buried it. That is the life of the homeless. We don't know when we will die." He was nine years old, talking like he was 90 years old. He saw no future.

"You're young," Songmi's mother softly said to Hyuk. "How can you be thinking like that?"

"That's nothing. Because it is true," Hyuk said, his voice slightly rising, motioning with his hands. He had seen a lot. "It isn't shocking. When people die here, I can only hope they will be born rich in the next life." This was Songmi's introduction to the lives and deaths of the homeless. He continued, "The most shocking thing: there are many times that I have seen people stealing clothes and shoes from the homeless who have just died. I even did it. I said to the dead body, 'I'm so sorry that you died, but I want to be alive.' Then I took his shoes and ran. I could not look back. I felt like the dead body might chase me."

～

THEY WERE STRUGGLING to survive when a homeless woman asked Songmi's mother, "Do you want to make some money?" The woman warned her that it would be dangerous and that it would be better for Songmi to wait at the train station. One day passed by, then another without Songmi eating at all. She went to a restaurant in front of the train station.

"Please, get out!" is the way she was greeted. "We don't have any free food."

"Can I drink some water? I'm so hungry." Songmi couldn't bring herself to ask for food. Songmi turned around and saw a bowl of leftover noddle soup. She asked the restaurant manager: "Can I have that?"

"Whatever!"

That bit of noodle soup gave her the strength to walk.

She started to feel delirious. Every woman she saw seemed to look like her mom. Starving, tired, and exhausted, Songmi sat down. "When is Mom coming?" Songmi sat outside of the train station.

Her mom ran inside the train station. She was asking others, "Have you seen a small girl about this size?" Songmi squinted at her. Her mother was panicking because Songmi hadn't been at the place she had left her.

Songmi saw her. "Mom," Songmi said. But it came out as a pathetic whisper. Her mom spun around and saw Songmi. "I'm sorry I'm late. I made some money, we can eat." She had made some money selling some of the potatoes they had stolen. She fed one of the small potatoes to Songmi, but she threw them up.

"I'm so sorry I can't prepare good food for you. I am trying so hard to give you a good life, but I am failing."

Songmi was happy to be with her mother again. "I'm grateful for everything you do for me."

Her mom said, "I will make some money for you so you can eat something good."

From then on, her mother would eat the small potatoes and save the good ones for Songmi. Her mother had an iron stomach — she could eat anything — but her daughter hadn't taken after her in that way. The next time they went stealing, they targeted garlic. It was more valuable, but also more difficult to steal. They were successful again, so they made more money. Her mother had decided not to take Songmi with her because of the danger that came with stealing food. Guards and farmers were protecting crops and getting more aggressive and abusive. One time when her mother failed to steal garlic, she came back with bruises all over her face. Her mom tried to hide her face, trying not to let Songmi get a full view of her. Songmi kept asking her what had happened.

"Last night, three of us went to steal garlic. A dog started barking, then a man appeared with a flashlight. We started running, but one guard caught me, and another guard caught the other woman. They started beating us and took our bags with everything we had."

A few days later, the couple who had gone stealing garlic with Songmi's mother said they wanted to try again. Her mom wasn't interested: "Shut up, no way." But seeing her daughter starving changed her mind. "Whatever. Let's try again."

They decided not to try stealing garlic again. Potatoes were less valuable and less protected. Songmi saw the three of them returning, laughing. They were smiling, and Songmi was smiling, too. This time, her mom didn't get hurt. The potatoes were small but better than nothing. The four of them went to the market to buy some *soondae*, blood sausage.

They were going to go out stealing again that night. Songmi gave them what she considered to be great advice: "Run faster if someone tries to catch you."

Laughing, her mother promised to be more careful. "Yes, I will run faster this time!" But they didn't run fast enough. Songmi waited, but for two days they didn't return. After the third day, only her mom returned that evening. She was covering her face and again she had no bags. Her mom told her the story that they had been happily grabbing potatoes. It seemed to be a little too easy.

Then they heard: "Hey! Stand up! Finally, we caught you thieves!" The guards had appeared out of nowhere. They had been hiding in a hole, listening. They had their flashlights off as they crept up on the latest food thieves. The trio of thieves made a run for it, but the two women were caught immediately and got beaten by the guards.

"Take off your clothes. Give us your bags." The two women gave them everything except their underwear. "Now, get in the hole. You can't go home." They crawled into the hole. The two men then went into the hut, talking. When her mom and the woman thought the men were sleeping, they decided to try to escape. Songmi's mom boosted the other woman first.

The guards woke up, but the other woman got away, wearing only her underwear. Songmi's mom was still trapped inside the dark underground jail. She could barely breathe, and she was thinking about her daughter being all alone at the train station. In the morning, the guards helped her out of the underground jail. They gave her back her clothes, but not the bags she used to steal potatoes. One guard asked why she hadn't escaped too.

She said, "I tried, but it wasn't easy." The guards told her to leave before they beat her again.

Songmi's mother had been badly beaten and struggled with returning. When she returned to find her daughter starving, she wondered about her strategy of leaving Songmi alone at the station. When Songmi was younger, her mother had been able to leave her with relatives or neighbors. But now, homeless at the train station, Songmi could be in greater danger by herself. The next day, as they were sitting on a bench in the train station facing each other, her mother reached out to hold both of her hands. She looked into her eyes. "My baby, tonight we are going to try to steal garlic. I will take you with me. They might beat just me, not you, because you are young. Let's try together — let's die together. I can't leave you here alone."

This would be Songmi's first time going stealing with her mother. She was seven years old. She was anxious and frightened, but she felt relieved to be joining her mother. It was around 7 p.m., dinner time, but they were starving and had nothing to eat. "Let's go," her mother said. She had a small bag with her to carry the garlic if they were successful. Songmi was holding her mother's hand as they walked together for about two hours. Her mother was usually talkative, making jokes. She would always laugh at whatever Songmi said. There were no jokes that night as they walked in silence. Songmi could sense that her mother was afraid and looked embarrassed to be bringing her daughter to steal with her.

"Songmi-ya, you are not going to steal the garlic; you are just going to hide outside. You need to wait for me. My baby, I am so sorry. You were born into the wrong family. If you had been born into a nice family, then you would not have to do this. Forgive me for taking you. In the next life, I hope you can be born into a nice family."

"Mom, it's okay. I am so happy to be with you. I am so proud of you. You are my mom. I would be born as your daughter again."

Her mother hugged her. A few minutes later, she quietly told her that they had arrived. Songmi looked around and saw there was a hill on one side, a few houses on the other side. Her mother pointed to a house. "There's garlic there. We need to wait for the people to go to sleep." They walked up the mountain, looking down at the houses. When it got cold, her mother handed her jacket to Songmi. They were watching the lights in the distance. Finally, the lights went off. They continued waiting. Her mother made the decision.

"Songmi-ya, now I should go. Stay here, don't go anywhere. I will be back in about 30 minutes. You may be able to see me. You can watch my shadow moving."

Songmi waited. Time was moving so slowly as she watched, trying to see her mom's shadow. She was hoping to hear her mom's footsteps. Then suddenly, her mom appeared. "Songmi-ya, let's go."

"Mom, did you do it? Where's the garlic?" She had left it at the base of the hill because it was heavy. They got down to the bottom of the hill, grabbed the garlic, and then walked quickly to get away. They occasionally looked back, to see if anyone was following them.

"Songmi-ya, I think you are good luck for me." They went directly to the market at 4 a.m. Merchants arrived early to meet the sellers who had been stealing during the night. Merchants could buy things at cheap prices from eager sellers. One of the early bird buyers came to Songmi and her mother, asking what they were looking to sell.

They had fresh garlic, just pulled out of the ground a few hours before. After they sold the garlic, it was time to eat. Songmi had not eaten in almost four days, only a few sips of noodle soup. It was probably then about 7 a.m., so they would have to wait another 90 minutes to two hours for the food market to open so they could eat.

They found a restaurant selling *soondae*. Songmi inhaled the food.

7

"DON'T EVEN TRUST YOUR BACK"

In the day-to-day life at a North Korean market, things were very tough. There was nothing glamorous. It was about survival.

The food market ran parallel with the river. Songmi and her mom were squatting and eating dumplings right below the food merchants. Their backs were to the river. Her mom, sitting to her left, said, "Songmi-ya, be careful, hold your food tightly. Some homeless people will grab food and run. In life, and especially here, don't even trust your back."

At the market, the homeless would grab anything. Food. Money. Grains. Clothes. Anything they could use, eat or sell, they would grab and run. Songmi nodded that she understood, then started eating using her hands, not chopsticks. It was too dangerous to use chopsticks as it would be much easier for a homeless person to grab her food off the chopsticks. Songmi took a bite, then as she was chewing, holding the dumpling with both hands near her mouth, a homeless person swooped in, as fast as a bullet, swiped the dumpling out of her hand, and took off running. Songmi turned her head to see that young man, probably in his late teens, had already dashed off.

"Mom," Songmi said, astonished. Her hands were still in front of her mouth as if she were still holding the dumpling. She looked at the homeless person who had stolen her dumpling. He had already swallowed the dumpling in one gulp. She looked at her hands. She looked at her mom. Her mom, always direct, showed no sympathy. She always wanted to teach Songmi how to protect herself. She loved Songmi, but she would tell her what she thought she needed to hear. "See! I told you. Hold it tightly." Songmi tried to explain, but her mother didn't want to hear it. She gave a frustrated sigh, then said, "Let's buy another one."

There was no banking system where Songmi lived. No credit cards. It was cash, barter, or promises. People must protect themselves even when they are counting money at the market. Homeless people will grab money even as it is being counted. North Koreans about to purchase something in the market will do their best to shield the money away from others as they are counting it. North Korean bills were often taped together to look whole. But that could mean a 1,000 won (0.90 USD) bill gets taped to a 5,000 won bill that has the same shape. People will trade with others who have the other half of the bill so they can be properly taped together. People do their best to hide their wallets, putting it on a string or chain. That way, if anyone tries to grab it, they will feel it. Others have underwear with pockets in them, so to get their money, they need to slightly pull their pants down to get their wallets.

Two well-dressed young men, probably in their early 20s, were following an older woman who was looking to buy something. They were pretending to look around as one slid the money out of her pocket, then handed it to his partner. She then felt in her pocket that her money was missing. She began shouting with a bewildered expression on her face, "Thief! Please, someone, help me catch the thief." Several people, including Songmi, saw what had happened, but no one said anything. Instead, they took a step back and avoided getting involved.

The woman pointed at the young man who was still there. "You! You stole my money!"

He held up his hands, 'I didn't steal anything. You can search me." She checked his pockets and clothing, but she didn't find anything. His partner had already disappeared from the scene.

This kind of thing happened often. No one was surprised about this or almost anything else that happened at North Korea's markets. Farmers visiting the market were willing to sell for whatever they could get so they could get back to their farms. They usually walked three to five hours to get to the market, meaning that going to the market was a full-day event.

Their desperation to sell for whatever they could get as quickly as possible meant it was easier for them to be cheated. One trick that Songmi witnessed many times would start with a buyer saying he or she didn't have enough cash on hand. As the buyer and farmer were negotiating, the buyer would have a partner secretly switch the bags. The buyer would then leave to supposedly get more money. After one or two hours, the farmers would be waiting, unaware that they had been deceived. Finally, they couldn't wait any more. They would try to find someone else to buy their rice or grains. They would open the bag to find mostly sand.

The same thing happened to Aunt Seonhui a few

years later. When she got back from the market, she said, "The world is going crazy. They will even steal your eyes if you are not watching. If you are selling something at the market, don't blink."

Songmi was selling food one day and had various foods in a big bowl. She had to keep it covered with plastic so homeless people wouldn't steal what she was trying to sell. But then, she needed to use the toilet. She asked the merchant next to her to watch her food. The woman told her, "No. It is better for you to take the food to the toilet with you. Think about it. If the homeless try to steal your food, I can't chase after them. If I do chase the person, then others will come and steal my food. I must watch my own food. I can't watch yours too. And if police show up, what can I do?"

Songmi carried her bowl of food into the toilet with her. She had different kinds of fried food to sell. She went to the toilet, but the toilet stall was too small. Sitting on the toilet, she left the door ajar. The food was close enough that she could reach it. If she heard someone approaching, then she would reach out to hold the bowl.

8

SIR

Songmi and her mother had been homeless for about six months when Songmi had a new problem. Her mother developed a relationship with a man who was often hanging out at the train station. Eight-year-old Songmi sized up this new man and didn't like what she saw. His face looked funny. When he smiled, which he always seemed to be doing, his eyebrows would point straight up. He wasn't a complete stranger to her mother. He had lived in Songmi's hometown and knew Songmi's mother in passing from that time.

He had been sent to the notorious Yodok prison. The prisoners there couldn't move and were forced to sit on their knees all day, except for when they ate. If they dared to scratch an itch or even move their heads, a guard watching them on camera would call the prisoner to the front for a beating. He said he preferred prison when he was forced to work hard. At Yodok, they couldn't move or see the sunlight. When he was released, he couldn't open his eyes for several minutes because he had not seen sunlight in a few years.

He said he felt so free when he was released, but he didn't have anywhere to stay. When he was in Yodok, his wife had brought him some food. While chewing, he found there was a note inside. She had written on it: "Let's get a divorce." Using a needle, he stitched his response on the back side of the paper she had given him. His message: "Do as you wish." She didn't think he would be able to get out of that prison. He was not interested in fighting it, and he knew she would have a tough life as the wife of a convict. He agreed to the divorce. But, as luck would have it, on the next day, the birthday of the dictator, he was released as part of an amnesty.

As he got healthier, he would be at the station playing cards with people, waiting for the next train, or for trains stranded because of electrical delays. He was always at the center of attention. He always seemed to be winning the card games. A lot of people would watch him, trying to figure out what he was doing. He was a magician with the cards. Some would get angry and storm off saying they would return later. Some would just concede to him.

He seemed to remember every card he played and even seemed to be able to guess which cards the others were holding. He would arrogantly play his cards while challenging others. Even when he didn't have a winning hand, he would bluff others, not with a poker face, but with his endless humor and bragging. Others standing behind him would say, "Hey! Are you sure you are going to win with that hand?"

"Shut up! I'm going to kill them all with these cards. One time, two times, three times," he would say, pointing at the others. "These cards will kill the others here."

This card player began talking to Songmi's mom. After catching up on each other's lives, they began talking about cooperating to make and save money together. After he made money destroying the others at cards, he would buy food for Songmi and her mother. Songmi didn't know at that point what kind of relationship he was building with her mother.

A few times when there weren't train delays or many passengers at the train station, he and Songmi's mother would go out stealing together. He wouldn't let Songmi join them; she had to wait at the station. He had some authority so he could arrange for Songmi to be protected. He seemed to know so many things about the world. For the first time in a long time, Songmi wasn't starving. Songmi's mother had been vulnerable when she went stealing with other homeless people. It was every man or woman for him or herself. It was different with the card player. If they got caught, he would be the one to fight, negotiate, or magically make them disappear from the scene.

Songmi's mother asked her what she thought. "Do you know the man who is playing cards and almost always wins? What if we get together? What if he becomes your new father?" Mother and daughter were sitting on a bench in the train station. Songmi was frowning. She shook her head to show her frustration. "No, Mom." Songmi's mom weakly tried to make a case for him, but Songmi didn't want another stepfather. Her mom let it go.

A few days later, the card player bought them food and gave her mom some money. Songmi was eying him suspiciously. She was wondering if they had already started a relationship. She asked her mom, with one finger on her chin, looking her mom directly in the eyes. "Mom. What's going on with that guy? Mom?"

"Nothing."

"Are you sure? He also gave you some money."

"I'm sure. He's just helping us."

Songmi was happy that he had given them some food. But she sensed that something was going on. Her mom still wasn't ready to completely confess. She usually told it like it was, but in this case, she was being evasive. "He wants to help us and have a good relationship together."

Songmi wasn't finished investigating. "That means..." Songmi's voice faded, waiting for her mother to finish the sentence.

"Let's just try."

Songmi could see what was about to happen. She could see that he was now her mom's boyfriend. Songmi didn't trust him. She had only had terrible father figures. With the new relationship, her mom and the card player were talking about the future, making and saving money, and buying a house together. Songmi saw another side to him, but she still wasn't ready to trust him completely.

"From now on," he said, "I will play cards every day, but that is just pocket money. We will also need to steal food. If we make a little money, then we can start selling things."

He would make money playing cards when there were people at the station. They went out to steal food about five times without getting caught, then sold much of what they had stolen. After more than a month, he said, "Okay, I think we have enough, we don't need to steal food again. We can't live like this long-term, we need to find a place to stay."

They moved in with an older woman who had been living alone and needed someone to care for her after she suffered a stroke. Ms. Shin slept in the bedroom, while Songmi, her mother and the card player slept in the living room. Songmi refused to call this new stepfather "Dad." Instead, she called him "Sir."

One day, Songmi's mom told her to prepare the dinner table. Songmi enjoyed having that family chore. After being homeless for months and starving so many times, she enjoyed having a home with food. She was setting the table when Ms. Shin sat down before Songmi had finished getting things ready. Songmi politely asked Ms. Shin if she could move so she could finish setting things up. She refused to move.

"No! I'm a grandmother, you shouldn't tell me to move." When Songmi's mother asked her what was going on, Songmi explained that she needed to set the table, but that Ms. Shin wouldn't move. Her mom got angry and threw a heavy stick used for washing clothes. Songmi started to sit down just as her mother tossed the stick. It hit Songmi right on her upper lip.

The quiet little tug-of-war between Songmi and the elderly woman had led to Songmi bleeding profusely from the mouth. Sir sprang into action. He didn't say anything, he picked up Songmi and carried her to a small clinic nearby.

Songmi couldn't talk. She was looking up at the sky that seemed to be moving as he carried her. She could only hear his breathing. This was the one time that Sir was serious. The clinic was wrapping up for the day. Sir asked them to check on Songmi, but the clinic was too small and unable to handle her case. He then carried her home and told them to get ready to take her to a hospital. Songmi had hated Sir and refused to accept him as her dad, but he was the one most desperate to save her at this moment. The blood from her lip was on Sir's shirt. For the first time, his eyebrows were straight, not pointing up.

And, for the first time, he showed anger to Songmi's mother.

He was ready to take Songmi to the bigger hospital, but her mother said it would take too long, about two hours. Songmi's mother tried to care for her lip with soybean sauce. That was her mom's home remedy for everything. It seemed that Songmi's mom didn't need to hear what the health problem was. She would already be reaching for the soybean sauce. If Songmi had broken her arm, her mother might have put soybean sauce on it. She put soybean sauce on Songmi's lip, which stung a lot.

Sir was angry at Songmi's mom. "You can't do that kind of thing, you need to be patient. You can't just throw things when you get angry. She is a girl, not a man."

"Whatever."

Sir was usually chatty in the house, but that night, he didn't say much. He went out to smoke. The incident had a major impact on Songmi. She felt that he was on her side. She began to think that Sir might be different from the other father-figures.

Sir was also influencing Songmi's mother. She was not the type to explain herself. On this occasion, however, she did explain herself. She was angry at Ms. Shin, but she couldn't attack her. She didn't want to hurt Songmi, so she just threw the stick but without using any power. She believed in disciplining her child and teaching her that she must be polite to elders. She had been raised that way and had been beaten often in her first marriage. Sir made it clear she could still be stern without physically punishing her. He said he wasn't going to tolerate her throwing things. His eyebrows were not pointing up when he said it. He was never violent or aggressive, he used his sharp wit and humor. Songmi's mom never again whipped or hit Songmi after that incident.

The apology from her mother still took time, but it did happen almost two years later. "I didn't mean to hurt you; I am so sorry."

SIR HAD TRULY TAKEN over the role of father and leader of the family. He teased everyone, especially Songmi. He would even tease her about the wound on her lip. Instead of her being ashamed, she even learned to joke about it. Her mother had put a bandage with soybean sauce on it. After about a week, she could talk again. She told her mother that with her big, wounded lip, she looked like an American.

Sir embraced the joke more than Songmi wanted. "Yeah! She looks like the enemy." He began telling stories about Songmi being a hated American.

"Hey! Don't say that!" Songmi said. She had made the joke, but he was taking it too far.

He teased her endlessly. "Can anyone understand you now? It seems that you have wind going through your mouth." When she would say something, he would repeat it, but with a muffled voice and a strange look on his face. He wouldn't stop teasing her about her wounded lip.

"Sir, stop it!"

At breakfast, lunch or dinner, he would be looking at her mouth, trying to figure out how to tease her. She would glare at him, knowing that he was looking for a way to tease her. As she ate she would have one or both eyes on him. When his eyebrows went up then Songmi knew the teasing was about to start.

"Oh," he said. "You can eat food. You look like a grand-mother the way you are chewing."

"See, I knew you were going to say something. I'm not a grandma."

"Oh, you're not a grandma. Maybe you are a goat?" Sometimes, it seemed that he would eat quickly just so he could focus on teasing Songmi. For the first time in a while, Songmi and her mother were in a stable family situation. Still, Songmi called the card player "Sir," not "Dad." He would say, "It doesn't matter, you can call me anything."

No matter what Songmi said or did, he would smile and joke. When they were sitting at the kitchen table, Songmi would frown or even glare at him. But he didn't complain, he would just have fun and tease her even more. Her birth father had always been cold to her. Her previous stepfather had started off nice, but then he began to be cruel to her. Maybe Sir would turn against her one day also.

However, she couldn't deny that her mother had a good relationship with him. She was constantly laughing about the things he said and did. Songmi was happy about that, she was starting to think he might not be another terrible father.

Everyone, except Songmi, laughed at his jokes. Her mother would have tears running down her cheeks as she laughed. Ms. Shin, who couldn't move around very well, would be slapping the floor, laughing. Songmi still had a stone face when she looked at Sir, but she was hiding that she was warming up to him. He always seemed to be plotting something to entertain her. One day he called out to her.

She was feisty. "What? I don't want to look at you!"

That wasn't completely true. When she saw those eyebrows go up, she did want to laugh. She didn't want him to know it, however.

"Just come over and look at me. Just look at my hand." He was rolling some paper into a small ball. He placed his hand flat, then he began pretending to push the ball of paper through the back of his hand. Songmi's eyes were following the movements, trying to figure out what the stupid magic trick would be. He was grunting and apparently hurting himself a lot trying to push the paper ball through his hand. Then, he pointed. "Songmi-ya! Look over there!"

Songmi looked, but she didn't see anything special. When she looked again, she saw that he was still rubbing his hand. Then, magically, the ball was under his palm rather than on top of his hand. "No way!" Songmi said. But she couldn't explain his magic. She had doubted his tricks when he was at the train station, but she was now seeing them directly rather than as part of a crowd. Now he was trying his tricks on her. "Do it again!"

He asked for more paper. Songmi rolled the paper into a ball to make sure he didn't do any tricks with it. She handed the small ball of paper to him as she watched him closely. Her eyes zeroed in on his hands and the ball of paper. He was pushing and rolling the paper around the top of his hand. He suddenly pointed up. "Oh, Songmi-ya, what's that?" Songmi looked up, but then her eyes quickly glanced back down at Sir's hand. She saw him about to move the ball from the top to the palm of his hand. She had caught him in the act.

She asked, "Is the ball still there?" She kept watching him. He was trying to figure out how to distract her, but nothing he did was working.

"Wait, wait," he said as he leaned over to the side, slightly lifting his butt off the floor. He was straining, counting "1...2...3. Okay, okay, almost..."

Bbbbbungggg.

He farted. Loudly. It felt like a tsunami had hit the entire room. Songmi looked away for a moment, waving her hand to fight the smell. "Dad! Go to the toilet!" For the first time ever, she called him Dad. It wasn't exactly a beautiful moment.

"Finally," he said. "That's it, I needed to do that." He resumed pushing the ball through his hand. When he finished grunting as he pushed down on his hand, he showed her that it had gone through. Songmi wasn't having it. He was pointing and doing so many things to distract her. Did his magic only work when she wasn't looking? "Dad. Do you think I'm an idiot?"

"See, it's real," he said. His eyebrows were still pointing up, but he had been cornered. "The ball went through my hand. See, it hurts." He was rubbing his hands to show how difficult it had been. Was he a better liar, actor or magician?

"Dad, where's the blood?" Songmi's hands were folded across her chest. She knew she had him. He insisted that it was magic.

"Let me have the ball," Songmi said, "I will show you magic." Songmi was copying him, rolling the ball around the top of her hand. Then with a surprised look on her face, she looked behind him. "Dad, what's over there?"

His eyebrows didn't move. His eyes didn't move. He stared directly at Songmi's hand. She tried again. "Dad! Who is she?" as she looked over his shoulder. He didn't blink. Songmi's mom was laughing. For the first time, all three of them were laughing together. When Songmi said "Dad," it wasn't forced, and she meant it.

SONGMI HAD TRIED to hate her new stepfather, but he was doing everything he could to make her love him. She thought to herself, "This is what a dad should be like. Someone to have fun with. Someone to care for you when you are in pain. Someone to be patient, even when you are angry at him." Songmi even began to laugh at his teasing. As Songmi began to laugh, he would joke and tease even more. He had lost his wife and children when he was in jail, but he now had a wife who loved him and a daughter who was starting to love him. Nothing was sacred, everything could be laughed about. He was plotting again.

"Songmi-ya, let's play a magic game."

Songmi was softer to him, but still, she didn't believe in his magic. She had caught onto his first magic trick. "No, Dad, I'm not an idiot. I'm not a baby. Your games are for three-year-old babies."

"This time, it is real. This is a new game." He put his hand on a small blanket.

"Dad, wait. Don't point anywhere," she said as she pointed up at the door. "And don't fart. If you fart, I am going to run out of the room."

"I can't promise that," he said. "Even the police can't stop someone from farting." He had about 15 cards under his fingers and thumb of his left hand. The cards were spread out. He said he would lift all the cards with one hand.

"That's not possible, and I don't trust you, Dad." She

said it, but her eyes were glued to his hand. He started pressing down with his right hand on top of his left.

"One, two..." All of the cards were moving up along with his hand. It seemed that the cards were floating under his hand. She was mesmerized.

She thought to herself, "This time, it may be real magic." He hadn't tried to divert Songmi's attention this time. She was feeling his hand to see what he was doing. She then tried it herself, but the cards didn't stick to her hand. For about two months, it was a big mystery in the house about how Dad could pick up cards with just one hand. When Songmi was alone, she tried that magic trick, but she couldn't pick up the cards. It seemed that her dad really had performed a magic trick.

One day, one of her dad's friends came to visit. He was playing the same magic trick. Songmi pleaded with him, "Please, please, show me how you do it." A magician doesn't show his tricks, but finally he relented. Songmi was not about to lose this chance to find the secret to her dad's magic.

Dad's friend asked, "Do you have a needle?"

Without answering, Songmi ran. "Mom! Where's a needle?"

She was cooking in the kitchen. "Look around, you can find one. Look in the drawer." Songmi looked around the drawer, then yes, she found a needle! She gave it to him. He showed her that he put the cards between the needle and the palm of his hand. Then, like magic, he picked up the cards.

Songmi said, "Uncle, please don't let Dad know you taught me this. I am going to play this with him." She couldn't wait for her dad to return home that day. "Dad, please, come and sit. Let's do some magic." He had gotten used to her asking him to show her some magic. His eyebrows were pointing up as he thought about which trick to show her.

"No, Dad, I'm going to do it." The tail was now wagging the dog.

He turned his head sideways with one eyebrow raised. She played the same magic trick on him. Her hand was small, so she could only lift nine cards. Her dad asked, "Who taught you?"

But her mother didn't know the trick. "Wow! How did you do it?" Dad and daughter kept the secret. For the first time, Songmi had a dad she could laugh and joke with, get teased by, and even endure his untimely and terrible farts. His eyebrows would be pointing up as he laughed and joked about everything. Her birth father had been a cold man who rarely acknowledged her. Her stepfather had regarded her as a child laborer. At last, Songmi had both a mom and a dad who loved her.

9

GONE FISHING

Songmi's parents bought a small unit in a "harmonica house" in the Shinsang-gu area where she had been born. Such homes had four families living under one roof, with each unit typically having one room and a kitchen. It might not have looked special to most people, but considering that they had been homeless, it was a step up.

There had been other upgrades. For the first time in a long time, Songmi was wearing clothes that had been bought. Previously, her mother had sewn her clothes. Her parents had stopped stealing and were looking for money-making opportunities. They went down to the southern part of North Korea when they heard that some people were making money selling clams they had caught there.

A young woman named Jeong, the sister of a neighbor, moved in with Songmi to take care of her while her parents were away. Aunt Yeonhui, recently married, lived just a few minutes away from Songmi's family. Half of the money to buy her home came from Songmi's parents.

But all was not well. After several health setbacks,

Grandma Choi died of a stroke on April 15th, the birthday of the founder of North Korea. Her family's home situation had stabilized over the last year, then like lightening, almost everything in the house was gone. Uncle Geumcheol began visiting the home where Songmi was living. It wasn't long before he was stealing things such as bowls, the family's rice cooker, the TV, the bicycle, and even spoons. He would sell them so he could buy alcohol. At first, he was careful about taking things, but he got more brazen, knowing that only his young niece was trying to stop him.

Nine-year-old Songmi became the defender of the house. "You are a drinker! Don't take our things." One day, someone broke in and stole their remaining nice clothes and blankets. "Uncle! Please, don't come here again. We don't have any food now. You stole everything." He denied it, but Songmi continued complaining at him. Songmi's hands were on her hips, as she stared up at her uncle.

He tried not to look like a guilty man. "Songmi-ya, that wasn't me. Don't you remember that you have to let me in?" His speech was slurred, his eyes were red. He couldn't even focus on Songmi as he denied her accusations.

No longer homeless, Songmi was protecting her home. "Now we don't have anything. We don't even have bowls or water buckets." He said he couldn't remember. After drinking so much, he was probably telling the truth that he couldn't remember what he had done. Songmi was exasperated. "Don't ever come again, never ever."

Songmi was back to scavenging for grass. She and Jeong sold the nice grass and ate the rest. Songmi struggled so much during that time. One of the neighbors who had also been fishing for clams told Songmi's parents about what was going on. Songmi's mother sent word through a neighbor that she wanted Songmi to join them. Songmi had often gone looking for her mom, but in this case, she would be going to the southern part of North Korea for the first time. Also, for the first time, Songmi would be taking a train by herself.

She managed to board the train to Muncheon City in Gangwon-do on her own, but she was standing. There were five soldiers sitting down. "Hey, little one," one soldier asked her. "Where are your parents? Who is your guardian? Where are you going"

"I'm going to Muncheon City to see them. Could you please tell me when we get there?"

"Hey, come here, sit on my knee. We are getting off before then. But we will tell other adults to take care of you until you arrive there."

The soldiers were singing, dancing and having fun on the train. "Hey, little one, can you sing for us?" They applauded Songmi as she sang. Songmi ate lunch and dinner with them. She was lucky that the soldiers helped her and that the electricity didn't go out during the trip. When the soldiers got off the train, they asked a woman sitting behind them if they could watch over Songmi until she arrived at Muncheon City the next morning.

"Thank you so much," Songmi said, waving enthusiastically to the woman who had looked after her the rest of the trip. Leaving the train station, she had no idea which way to go, but she was now a veteran of looking for her mom. She asked many people how to get there. She got really lucky; two women were headed in the same direction. She got worried when they took her through the mountains. Others pointed her in a different direction. Songmi asked if they were going the right way.

"This is a shortcut. If you don't go this way, you might not arrive until the evening."

When they said goodbye, they pointed out the area she needed to go to find her mom. She started walking, but then when she thought about seeing her mother, she began running. She would slow down to ask others if she was going in the right direction. A farmer pointed to a few houses, telling her, "You want to go to the one in the middle."

After an elderly woman opened the door, Songmi said her name, then asked if she could see her mom. The elderly woman said she would be back soon, but Songmi was truly her mother's daughter. "Grandma, can I go see my mom?"

She laughed. "Okay, let's go see your mom." They walked for a few minutes. Songmi saw many people in wetsuits holding onto tubes, bobbing up and down in the water. The elderly woman said, "I can see your mom. She's not wearing a cap."

Songmi saw her. "Mom! Mom!" Songmi waved her hands frantically. She rolled up her pants and walked into the water.

"Little one, be careful, there are many sharp things in the water," the elderly woman said. "You have to wear something when you are in the water. Don't worry, your mom will come back soon, after she catches a lot of clams."

Songmi was playing in the water, waiting for her mom to come out. She could see her mom, dad and another person who was a neighbor come out of the water. She shouted to them. "I'm here!" They were all surprised and happy. "Wow, you made it!" Songmi was so happy to explain, and her parents and neighbors listened and laughed as she energetically told her story. They had some fresh fish for lunch. It had been a long time since Songmi had eaten rice and fish.

Songmi explained to her mom what was happening at their home. They had been robbed and her uncle was stealing things. They stayed together in Muncheon City for a month or two, her parents returned to Shinsang-gu to sell the house, and then returned to Muncheon City.

While her parents worked during the day and also handled family affairs, Songmi's entertained herself by climbing trees, lying down on the huge tree limbs, and listening to the cicadas. She felt so tall when she was in a tree. She could see everything and everyone—the trees and houses nearby, the birds and the cicadas. It felt so serene, like when she was back at her first home. She loved the sounds of the birds but hated the cicadas.

"Why don't I have wings? Then I could catch the cicadas and eat them. They are so noisy!" Songmi was still restless about not being able to go to school in this new area. She would be with her mom in the mornings and at night, but during the day, she was bored by herself. She still couldn't go to school, she didn't have any friends in the area, and she was isolated in the countryside. She was bored during the day and still wanted to go to school, but was happy being with her mom and dad.

10

MOM'S GONE, AGAIN

As clam season was winding down, Songmi's family first moved to Aunt Yeonhui's home short-term, then rented a home nearby. Songmi had gotten used to her mom disappearing for months at a time, but this time her mom was with her dad. She felt secure with him in their family. It was probably 2002 or 2003, and Songmi was at her Aunt Yeonhui's home waiting for her mother to return. Her mom was visiting by herself, so there were no magic tricks or teasing from Dad. Her mom would come and go, trying to make money in different ways.

One day, a neighbor told Songmi that her mom was waiting for her near Geumjin River. Songmi rushed to see her. "Why didn't you come into Aunt Yeonhui's house?"

"I can't go in, I don't have any money," her mother explained. "I really wish we could live together. I am sorry that you are staying with them." There was a time when her mother never apologized or explained things to her daughter, but that had changed. Songmi didn't care, she was delighted to be with her mom. She had no idea how long they would be together, so she was going to enjoy every moment.

Her mother then gave her some notes. "I wrote these, she said. "If someone says something bad, if you're uncomfortable or tired, please look at these; always remember that I love you." Songmi enjoyed that night, sleeping with her mom near the river. They were sleeping on the ground without any blankets, just a small scarf, but it felt so comfortable for Songmi. It reminded her of the time they were together in the barn. They listened to the radio until midnight.

Her mom loved writing poetry. "Songmi-ya, can you hear the radio? Sometimes I sleep outside like this. It makes me think about things. That's a good time for me to write."

Songmi then had the chance to give her mother a gift. "Mom, here is some money." Songmi was so proud of herself as she handed the money to her mom. It wasn't much, but it was a lot for a child to have, and enough to buy a few kilograms of rice.

"My goodness. How did you make this money?" Laughing, she asked, "Did you steal it?"

"No! I sold water when the trains stopped at the station."

"Your aunt didn't take it?"

"I gave her some, but I have been saving the rest of it for you."

"Your aunt is always trying to get money, are you sure she believed you?"

"I told her that no one was buying my water because so many people were selling it."

"I am so proud of you. I don't want this money," her mother said. "But I should take it because it will help me so much. Songmi-ya, I am so sorry. I want to live with you, and I want to take you, but I don't know how long I must keep living like this. Please, just wait a few months."

SONGMI WAITED SEVERAL MORE MONTHS, staying with Aunt Yeonhui. One day, Aunt Seonhui came to visit. She whispered to Songmi, "Your mom is at my house. She wants to see you." Songmi wasn't sure why it was a secret, but she sensed that she shouldn't announce that her mom was there. Songmi was so excited, she was ready to run to see her mom. Songmi told Aunt Yeonhui that she needed to visit Aunt Seonhui's house.

"Don't forget that it will be harvest time soon," Aunt Yeonhui said. She always reminded Songmi about work.

Songmi and Aunt Seonhui made the one-hour walk to her home. It was September 25, 2005, two days before Songmi's 12th birthday. Songmi cried as she hugged her mom for the first time in months. "Mom, you took so long to come back." Songmi was both joyful and complaining.

They talked, then her mother said, "The money you gave me helped so much." Songmi's mom handed her 10 times more than what Songmi had given her. "My baby, I wanted to give you this money because it will be your birthday in two days. You can buy a book or something delicious to eat." It was the perfect moment. Her mom had returned to her just before her birthday. Then her mom ruined everything. "I need to leave tomorrow."

"Oh, but my birthday is in two days, please stay with me."

"I'm so sorry, I must leave. Your dad is waiting for me to return." Songmi was thinking that they must be planning something big. But what could it be? Her mom gave her a knife next. "You can use it to make food." In particular, she was referring to *dubu bab*, or North Korean rice tofu, which required a knife to prepare. Next, she gave Songmi a multiplication table. She was worried because Songmi had only attended elementary school for a year and hadn't been in school for a while. "Please study this. When I come back on October 10th, I will check to see if you have learned how to multiply." She was the one person who was focused on Songmi's education.

Songmi hated to see her mom go, but she was happy to hear a specific date. Most of the time when her mother left, Songmi had no idea when she would return. In this case, Songmi could prepare for their next meeting. Songmi had new energy. Wherever she went for the next two weeks, she took that multiplication table with her and studied those numbers. She wanted to make her mother proud.

She could barely sleep the night before her mother was to return. While most people were celebrating the founding of the North Korea Workers' Party, Songmi was memorizing math to be prepared for her mother's test. The train station wasn't far from Aunt Seonhui's home; she could hear when a train was passing by.

Bbang-bbang! When she heard the train, she felt like her mom was calling her. She would run outside every day, wondering if her mom was on that train. Then, the big day arrived. October 10th. Songmi listened for the trains all day, but her mom wasn't on any of them. Every day after that, Songmi ran to check if her mom had arrived. She would hear the *bbang-bbang* sound, but her excitement turned to anxiety and her joy turned to tears every time she heard the train sound.

Sobbing, Songmi said, "Mom is not coming back. I want to go find her." Finally, Aunt Seonhui got frustrated with Songmi crying every day. Crying, her aunt hit Songmi on the side of her head. Aunt Seonhui looked at her and said, "Don't cry, your mom is not going to come back. So don't wait." Then her aunt said something Songmi wasn't expecting. "Your mom is not in this country. You don't need to wait for her."

"Don't wait? Mom isn't coming back? She's not in the country?" She looked at her aunt. "Mom promised me that she would come back on October 10th. She's not lying. I will still wait." Songmi couldn't stop crying. "Mom will return to me." Songmi didn't give up, she still went to the train station every day to check for her mom. She cried whenever she heard the *bbang-bbang* sound.

For almost a month, she still hoped that her mom would return. When Songmi opened her eyes in the morning, she would think about her mother. The *bbang-bbang* sound became a regular reminder that her mom was missing. Finally, Songmi gave up. "Aunt, I can't keep staying here. Mom is not in this country; I hope she is safe."

She returned to Aunt Yeonhui's house about an hour away from Aunt Seonhui's. Songmi cried most of the time as she walked. She had gone looking for her mother so many times, but now there was nowhere for her to look. It dawned on her that at the age of 12, she would be on her own. How would she live? She wondered if she could live by herself. Both aunts had let her stay with them when her mother was gone for extended periods of time, but now her mother might not even be in the country. As Songmi walked, she thought about the knife that her mother had given to her and how she could survive in this world without her mother. She thought that it might be easier for her to commit suicide.

A MAN KNOCKED on the door to deliver a letter to the home of Aunt Yeonhui. Songmi opened the letter. It was from her mom. She apologized to Songmi for not letting her know that she was going to China with Dad. She wrote that they were going to make money then return to North Korea. Dad's aunt was in China; he had gone there several times before. This time, he had taken Songmi's mom with him. Songmi was sad they were gone but also happy to know her mom was alive.

"You're not alone," Songmi said to herself. Her aunt had warned her not to wait for her mother, but when Songmi saw that letter, it confirmed in her mind that she was correct to continue waiting. Songmi was elated by the letter, but her aunt and uncle were angry. They had talked about being watched by neighbors because Songmi's mom had escaped from North Korea. A letter coming from China could result in more surveillance or even a visit from North Korean police investigating them. Songmi's mom was also taking a chance by sending the letter. The broker delivering it could have revealed her presence if he had gotten captured. The letter would have been evidence that could easily have led to her being executed if she had been repatriated to North Korea. Plus, because it mentioned that Dad had relatives in China, it also could have been evidence against him. The North Korean regime made even simple communication between families a crime.

Songmi later learned that her parents crossed the border into China on October 3, 2005. They had sent money to Songmi and Dad's two children but they couldn't confirm that the money had been delivered. Songmi's dad said he would return to North Korea to give money directly to Songmi and his children. Her mom was waiting for him. Songmi later heard that he had gotten captured at the border.

Mr. Yu Geunsang, the expert card player, magician, comedian, the stepfather Songmi originally hated but had learned to love and call Dad, the man whose eyebrows would always point up as he was laughing and joking, had been sent back to the Yodok prison.

11

FOOD IN THE PICTURE

Songmi was standing on a bridge over a small river near Aunt Yeonhui's home. The water was so beautiful and clear. She asked herself, "Should I jump in?" Songmi was already tired of life at the age of 12. Her mother was in China. Songmi had been moved from home to home and was then staying in the home of an aunt who probably didn't want her there. If she made a mistake, then Aunt Yeonhui would berate her or throw something at her.

"If I commit suicide, would they be happy?" She didn't know how to swim, so she knew she would drown if she jumped in or allowed herself to fall. She had one leg over the side as she held onto the bridge. "Would my aunt be happy? They could save money because they wouldn't have to take care of me. Why do I have such a tough life? Why did Mom give birth to me?" She thought about many things." She was crying, but there was no one there to stop her from jumping in. There wasn't even anyone to yell at her, "Hey you stupid kid, stop playing around."

She was waiting for someone to come by, to

discourage her from committing suicide, but she was still alone. Only one thing stopped Songmi from drowning herself. "What about when Mom comes back, and she finds that I am dead?" She had something to live for; she needed to be alive when her mom returned. "You are working so hard while you wait for your mom to return. Just wait a little more."

Songmi moved slowly, making sure she didn't fall or slip. A few minutes earlier, she had been dangling herself off the bridge. She would have to pull herself together until her mother returned. She was on the bridge for two hours and hadn't seen anyone. "See, no one cares about me. I will stay with my aunt so I can see Mom again." She went back to her aunt's home. Everyone was sleeping; no one had come out to check on her.

ONE DAY, Aunt Yeonhui spilled some rice as she was cooking. "If the mother is pretty, the daughter is also pretty." She muttered it to herself, but Songmi heard her. Songmi's mother was gone, not taking care of her daughter, so her aunt was criticizing Songmi's mother and saying that Songmi was not worth her effort.

Songmi lost her appetite. She skipped that meal and many others after that. It was another terrible reminder for her that she wasn't wanted, but that moment also made her realize that it wasn't enough for her to help around the house. "What can I do for her? If I stay here, I must do something for my aunt." Songmi had no money, no education, and no idea what to do.

Songmi watched Aunt Yeonhui that day. Her aunt bought wood every day so she could cook food to sell. She could help Aunt Yeonhui by collecting wood for her. When Songmi was younger she had tagged along with Uncle Geumcheol one day when he collected wood. She had also collected tree limbs for her mother when they lived in a barn together. Songmi asked a 17-year-old girl named Sunghee who was selling wood how she could also collect it. She told Songmi that she went to a mountain every day, collecting tree limbs she would then carry on her back. Songmi asked her if she could join her.

"What? You're too young." Sunghee was looking at this tiny girl, sure that she couldn't comprehend how difficult the work would be. It was tiring just getting to the mountain a few hours away. Then after scavenging for tree limbs, there was still the difficulty of hauling the wood back home or to a market. Grown men got exhausted from the grueling labor. How in the world would a tiny girl handle it?

Despite the warnings, Songmi was determined. "Please, I have to do it. I can't survive if I don't. I must stay here so my mom can find me." Songmi did her best to explain her desperate situation.

Sunghee reluctantly agreed, saying, "Okay, but don't make it too difficult on yourself."

That night, Songmi told Aunt Yeonhui that she would go to the mountain to get wood. Her aunt asked, "Are you sure you can do it?"

Songmi said, "I already asked Sunghee if I could go with her. She will take me tomorrow." Her aunt rarely smiled at her, but she did at that moment. Songmi realized that she had found a way to survive in Aunt Yeonhui's home. That was the true start of Songmi engaging in manual labor. Four days a week for the next five years, Songmi would walk about three hours to the mountain to collect tree limbs. It would take her about five hours to walk back carrying the tree limbs on her back. She was so tiny and carrying huge tree limbs on her back. People would say, "It looks like some wood is walking down the street."

Questions came at her from almost everyone who saw her. "Why are you doing this? Why are you working so hard? Where are your parents?"

Her aunt had doubted she could do such difficult work. When Songmi returned, her aunt gave her a huge smile.

Songmi cut one of her fingers one day. It wasn't just the pain and bloody glove that bothered her. What really made her sad is that she knew no one would be waiting for her when she returned to her aunt's home. Any concern that her aunt would have about her injury would be about whether Songmi could work the next day.

Everyone was sleeping when Songmi returned home after collecting wood. When she opened the door, the family dog, Allogi, was waiting for her. She jumped on Songmi, licked her face, and made her feel loved. Sitting outside with Allogi, Songmi looked up at the sky. "I miss Mom. Allogi, you are the only one who waits for me."

Songmi was little more than a child laborer. She took care of her aunt's children, did laundry, cleaned the house, helped cook dinner, did all kinds of farming, and sold food that her aunt had cooked. Going to school wasn't a consideration.

Aunt Yeonhui was happy at last, but it was short-lived. Songmi began to resent her aunt. She missed her mom, she wasn't going to school, and she was working hard all the time. She could hear her friends playing while she was working to survive. When Songmi started collecting wood, her aunt had been so happy. Every time Songmi took on a new household chore, her aunt would expect more.

She started selling water to passengers stranded at the train station. Her aunt was pleased but told Songmi that she should also sell food. With one hand, Songmi was selling food, with the other hand she was selling water. Somehow, she did it all without a third hand.

She rushed home to give the money to Aunt Yeonhui. She was so happy to get money from Songmi instead of having to spend it on her. Songmi saw that rare smile and heard that happy voice from her aunt. She was learning how to survive in her aunt's home.

It was a rare occasion that Songmi got to eat nice food with her aunt and uncle. Most days, the food she was selling and could smell around the house was just "food in a picture." She could see the food, she could touch the food, but she couldn't eat it. Her aunt and uncle would often wait until Songmi had gone to sleep, then they would eat. Songmi could smell the good tasting food as she went to sleep hungry.

Songmi started most mornings in the winter walking to the river with a stone and two buckets. Wearing gloves to protect her hands, she would repeatedly slam the stone into the ice. She would smile to herself when the ice would finally break. She was slamming the stone into the frozen water when she thought she heard the sound of a baby goat. *Ang-ang-ang*. Songmi stopped, started listening and looking around. She resumed slamming the stone into the frozen water, then heard the baby goat sound again. Then a third time.

Songmi left the buckets and stone there to investigate. She walked slowly, listening, walking in the direction of the sound. Looking ahead, she saw a small blanket flapping in the wind. The sound was coming from there. As she got closer, it sounded like a human baby, not a baby goat. "How could a baby be outside alone now? It is so cold!" Then she saw that it was a baby wrapped in a blanket.

When North Korean children ask about how they were born, their parents will often answer, "I found you under a bridge." But it was really happening. A baby had been left under a bridge. Songmi looked around, checking to see if anyone else was in the area. She unfolded the blanket to touch the baby. Cradling the still warm baby, she returned to her aunt's house.

Songmi explained, "I think the baby's mother abandoned her."

"Are you sure? Did you look around?"

"I did. But nobody was there, and the baby was crying."

Her aunt and uncle then turned against her. "Why did you bring the baby? You're causing a problem."

Causing a problem was something Songmi tried to avoid. She had become so passive in her life. "Aunt, it is so cold outside, the baby might die. I couldn't leave her there."

Aunt Yeonhui asked: "Where are the buckets?"

Songmi had left the two buckets on the water near the bridge. When she went back, they were gone. Songmi tried to explain. "I'm sorry. I thought it was a goat. But it was a baby. What could I do?" She had seen her aunt show more concern for their animals than she did for this baby that was in her home. If Songmi had found a goat, her aunt and uncle might have been happy to sell it.

Songmi said, "Okay, if no one takes the baby, then I will take care of her."

Her aunt glared at her. "Shut up! You can't take care of a baby. You are living in my house."

They took the baby to their area leader. The leader suggested they find someone struggling to conceive a baby. Aunt Yeonhui thought about her friend Myeong-sook who lived just five minutes away. Aunt Yeonhui sent Songmi to check with Myeongsook.

Songmi was frantically calling for her. Myeongsook came out, alarmed. "What happened?"

"You need to come to our house!"

Songmi briefly explained what had happened and Myeongsook said, "Wait, let me get dressed." They rushed to Aunt Yeonhui's home. Aunt Yeonhui offered her the chance to take the baby. Myeongsook said she needed to bring her husband. She returned a few minutes later with her husband.

"Where did you find the baby? Are you sure it is okay if we take her?" After hearing Songmi's full explanation, the couple said it might be a sign that they deserved to have a child.

Three years later, the baby's birth mother showed up. She asked if they had gotten her under the bridge. She wanted her baby back. The family said no. Myeongsook's family loved the baby and considered her to be their own. She asked if she could see the baby. They said no.

THERE WAS a knock at the door, a letter was being delivered from China. Inside the letter, Songmi's mother gave instructions for Aunt Yeonhui to go to Hyesan City near the border with China so she could send them money. Aunt Yeonhui's husband went to Hyesan City. He called Songmi's mom, telling her that she could send the money. There were many cases in North Korea of shady brokers cheating families or of desperate family members rushing to falsely claim money. Songmi's mother was confirming everything, including whether he was the real husband of Aunt Yeonhui.

Songmi's mother sent money to the Chinese broker handling the money transfer. He then gave it to the North Korean broker who gave it to Songmi's uncle several days later. Songmi's uncle returned to Shinsang-gu with three million won (about 2,500 USD). The next day, however, the North Korean government devalued the currency. The money that Songmi's mom had sent was worthless. Everyone needed to turn in their Korean won. In exchange, they could get up to about 90 USD. So many people had their life savings destroyed and Songmi heard that many people committed suicide. In anger, people were burning the money they had.

A few months later, Songmi's mother sent about 1 million won (835 USD). This time, Songmi's uncle received it in Chinese currency rather than North Korean Won. Many North Koreans had learned the lesson not to trust North Korean money. Songmi's life changed because of the money sent by her mother. Songmi would no longer have to collect wood. Her aunt still did not suggest, however, that Songmi resume going to school.

12

STEALING

Songmi and two of her friends were running. They had planned to steal some potatoes that night. One of her friends said, "I saw that there are some potatoes there. I don't see a guard." The three children studied the area. There were many potatoes there, ready to be dug up, taken and eaten. The three children — two girls and one boy — looked around, and they could see one small hut. Was anyone watching them?

It was about 9 p.m. They didn't have a hoe or any tools that would help them steal more potatoes. They used their bare hands. The three of them sat down, their heads were level with the potatoes. The potatoes seemed to be swaying as the children dug. Songmi had dug up about 10 potatoes. The other two had already dug up about 20 potatoes each that they had put in their bags.

A guard who had snuck up on them shined his flashlight. They had been caught, and there was no denying what they were doing. They had potatoes in their bags and soil all over their clothes. The guard started running in their direction.

"Hey! You little ground moles!"

All three children began running without the potato bags. He was yelling and cursing as he started chasing them. He then yelled the magic word: "Stop!" The other two children kept running and didn't look back. Songmi stopped running. She slowly walked back to the guard. He was furious. "Finally, I caught you, you little mole. What are your parents' names? Where do you live?" Songmi explained that she didn't have parents. "How many times have you come here stealing potatoes?"

"Today is my first time." When she was younger, she had dug up some potatoes and eaten them on the spot, and she had watched as her mother had stolen potatoes and garlic, but she had never run off stealing them.

"Are you sure?"

"Yes."

"I can see that, because you stopped running," he said. "Why did you stop?"

Songmi's answer was matter-of-fact. "Because you yelled for us to stop." Even when she could get punished, her mother had taught her that it was always better to tell the truth.

The guard who had been so angry burst out laughing. "Okay, come here, little mole." He shined his flashlight on the potato bags. "Which potatoes were you stealing?" Songmi could have lied and pointed at one of the other bags with many more potatoes, but she pointed at her bag.

He looked at her. "Why did you get only a few potatoes? Look at the other bags, they got many potatoes. You only got a few potatoes." He looked at her. It wasn't quite sympathy. Perhaps it was the acknowledgment that many people were stealing to avoid from starving. "I believe you, and this is probably your first time. You don't know how to steal, and you don't even know how to run away when you get caught." He gave Songmi the potatoes that she had dug up. "You were honest, so take the potatoes. But if you do it again, I won't let you get away. I got into trouble because people have been stealing potatoes. Now get out of here, don't ever come back here stealing again."

If they had met in a different time, place or country, he could have been a mentor or uncle to her. Instead, they were both trying to survive in North Korea.

"ARE YOU STUPID?" It was the next day, and the two other kids were talking to Songmi near the river. "Why did you stop running?"

Songmi countered, "Why did you run?"

"What?" The boy, who was a year younger than Songmi, pointed at her. "She's stupid."

They were befuddled trying to understand Songmi. "Is this for real? The guard was there, so we had to run. We don't want to get into big trouble. Next time, we can't bring you with us."

Songmi still wasn't convinced. "That guard wasn't that scary. You left everything. I got 10 potatoes."

"You got lucky. You don't know how scary the guards can be."

Songmi got better at stealing. It seemed to be the way of life in her area. People would steal clothes even when they were drying. It didn't matter what it was, others would even steal underwear or socks.

The two friends gave Songmi another chance, but they warned her, "This time, keep running if there is a guard. Don't look back."

They all got away with cabbage. When she got back home with the seven heads of cabbage, her aunt and uncle asked where she got them from. She said, "I stole them."

They were thrilled because they didn't have to spend their money to buy the cabbage. Songmi was still trying to find ways to survive in her aunt's home. She realized that stealing food would make them happy. It was more comfortable for her to steal from strangers rather than to feel like a thief in her aunt's home. She was living for others, not for herself. Even her smile wasn't for herself. She had to let her aunt think at every moment that she was happy and thankful. She didn't feel welcome there, but it was still better than being homeless again. She had known homeless people who had starved or frozen to death at the train station.

Songmi was learning about the world of stealing food. Many different kinds of food got stolen. Grains, dry corn, potatoes, garlic, rice. But probably the number one food item stolen was kimchi. It is eaten at almost every meal from winter to spring. Kimchi was a target of food thieves for two main reasons.

One, there were few refrigerators in North Korea when Songmi was there. She never saw one, she only heard about them. That meant that kimchi was stored in a jar underground or in a small warehouse. The food thieves could search around to find where it might be buried or check to see if the warehouse had been left unlocked.

Two, the strong smell. A food thief could be walking down the street, smell the kimchi, then make a U-turn, either to nab the kimchi then or to return later. When Songmi was homeless, she learned that many of the food thieves didn't have bags to carry things they had stolen. In some cases, they were so hungry and tired that they couldn't carry anything. They would locate the kimchi, take the lid off, and eat it right there, usually with their hands that might not have been washed recently.

Songmi remembered one time when Grandma Bae got ready to cook breakfast. She went outside to get the kimchi, but she saw there were no lids on the kimchi jars. "Did someone take the lids off the kimchi jars?" They all denied it. Songmi was too young, she wouldn't have been able to reach the lid, but she registered her denial anyway. They guessed that someone homeless used the lids to carry the kimchi away. Songmi's grandmother had to cover the jars with plastic and then blankets.

To please her aunt and uncle, and to have some extra food for herself, Songmi began stealing cabbage, potatoes and corn. But she never stole kimchi or rice. Those thieves got arrested and put in jail.

She knew that many soldiers stole kimchi. She would see them bring kimchi to her aunt to barter for other food. Her aunt never asked where the kimchi had come from. Sometimes the soldiers would steal animals and bring them to her aunt to barter. One time some soldiers brought a small pig. Her aunt and uncle suspected that the pig might have been stolen from next door.

Chickens were also targets for food thieves. Good thieves stole chickens in broad daylight by feeding them a few grains. A chicken might have been wary, but it couldn't resist something to eat. Then the chicken thief grabbed the chicken and put it in his or her backpack or bag.

In the countryside, people labeled their animals. There were many cases of people catching others who had stolen their chickens. In some cases, a neighbor might have just bought some chickens, not knowing they had been stolen or not knowing where they had been stolen from. Those chickens being sold on the spot were cheaper than at the market. If the chicken thieves wanted to make more money, they could go to the market. Most thieves didn't want to go far with a live animal. There were some cases of the same chicken being stolen and sold several times before it finally ended up on someone's dinner plate.

One day, a soldier sold a chicken to Aunt Yeonhui. After he left, a neighbor stopped by to buy some food. The neighbor spotted her chicken walking around.

Aunt Yeonhui denied it. "What are you talking about? I bought it a few hours ago."

"That is my chicken." The neighbor told Aunt Yeonhui to go with her to her home. She then showed her that the chicken's legs were all wrapped with a red string. Songmi's aunt couldn't deny it. The neighbor took her chicken.

Aunt Yeonhui learned a lesson. Whenever people brought an animal to sell, whether it was a chicken, a rabbit, or a pig, she would investigate it. She had no problem with buying a neighbor's chicken. She just wanted to make it more difficult to identify. If there was a string on it, Aunt Yeonhui would cut the string.

WHEN SONGMI WAS ABOUT 15, her aunt bought a piglet as an investment for the family. Her uncle built a container using lumber from trees. Aunt Yeonhui heard about a neighbor's pig getting stolen. Her aunt and uncle were trying to figure out ways to protect the pig. "I can't sleep,"

Aunt Yeonhui said several times. "I'm worried that someone might steal the pig."

After hearing her say it several times Songmi guessed what her aunt wanted. Songmi asked, "Should I sleep with the pig?"

"Can you?" Her aunt smiled.

At that point, Songmi preferred the pig over her aunt and uncle. She, her aunt, uncle, and two babies were sleeping together on the bed in one room. She still felt like an outsider to the family. Her aunt and uncle were eating secretly so they wouldn't have to share with Songmi. Even when they didn't finish eating something, they would store it without sharing any with Songmi.

Songmi's new sleeping area was right above the pig's. Because of Songmi's body being there, no one would be able to open the door to steal the pig. She would sleep there even when it rained. She had a blanket, and her clothes were rolled up to make a pillow. Those clothes were worn-out, with holes at her elbows and knees, but they were better than no pillow at all. She still would have preferred her mom's arm as a pillow. She often looked up at the stars, counting them, and thought about her mom. She would listen to the radio until the programming went off. When the host of the show would read a novel, she felt like her mom was reading to her.

The pig became Songmi's new listening partner. "Are you happy? You are always eating something. They feed you more than they feed me. I want to be like you. You are more important than I am in this family."

Pigs had been among her favorite animals but living with one was different. One problem was the smell. "Hey, Pig, don't poop," she would tell the pig. "It smells so bad." Holding her nose, she regularly cleaned up after the pig.

Sometimes Songmi would battle with the pig, using a stick to scare it. The pig would catch the stick with her mouth and chew. She was stronger than Songmi, so it was a real fight.

Hearing the commotion, Aunt Yeonhui asked from the house, "What are you doing with the pig?"

Songmi answered, "She made me angry."

"Seriously, are you fighting with a pig?"

Sometimes Songmi would scratch the pig's stomach as she had done when she was younger, but sometimes when the pig wouldn't sleep then she would hit the pig's stomach. "Be quiet, I need to sleep." Songmi still loved pigs, but not as much as she had before.

When the pig got heavy, her aunt and uncle sold her. "I miss my pig," Songmi said to herself. "Someone might be eating her right now. I had thought the pig was lucky because my aunt and uncle were feeding her so much, even more than they feed me. But now, I am happy I am not a pig."

With no pig, there was a new dilemma. Should Songmi start sleeping inside the house again with her aunt's family? There was no reason for her to sleep in the container with no pig there to guard, but she also didn't feel welcome in the home. About two weeks later, they got a new piglet. Songmi chose to sleep with the piglet instead of in the home with her aunt and uncle.

13

MICE AND EGGS

Songmi was sleeping one night when she woke up with a feeling that someone had entered the room. Had someone come into the house to steal something? Most thieves would take whatever was outside, so it was scary if someone was bold enough to enter a home. Songmi was home alone, sleeping in the house as her aunt and uncle had gone to visit her uncle's parents.

She looked around but she couldn't see anyone in the dark. "Am I dreaming?" A few minutes later, she heard what sounded like someone moving around. She was terrified. "Maybe someone is here," she thought. Alone and afraid, she said, "Hey! Don't move! I know you are there."

The sound stopped. She lit a stick so she could see. With the light from the stick, she could look around the room, but she didn't see anyone. "What's the sound?" she asked herself. There was complete silence again. She couldn't sleep. It seemed that someone was scratching.

"Who is it?" She said it out loud and to herself. She was afraid of the silence, but also afraid someone might answer. She lit the stick again and began to creep over to where she was hearing the sound. She saw the trespasser: a huge mouse. The mouse had a big stomach because it had been eating. It was trying to get back into the hole it had come in, but now its stomach was too big.

"Hum, you!" She grabbed the mouse's tail, but she didn't know what to do with it. The mouse turned around and bit into her right hand. Songmi slammed the mouse on the floor. The mouse was alive, but it could barely move. Songmi could see that her hand was bleeding, but she couldn't feel anything. She ran outside. It was midnight and she started screaming to her neighbor. "Aunt, there's something strange in our home!" Her neighbor came running out.

"What happened?"

"A mouse bit me! I can't feel my hand! I fought a mouse, and I was the loser!"

They went into her aunt's home. The mouse was in the same spot. It seemed that it had been injured. The neighbor grabbed the mouse, picked it up by the tail, and slammed it against the floor to kill it.

"Songmi-ya! Where's the soap? We need to clean your hand."

She was worried that Songmi may have been infected. Her hand was bruised and swollen, and her hand was already getting hard. She started rubbing Songmi's hand with soap. She couldn't feel it at first, it was like she was being scratched softly. Then Songmi yelped. "Too painful!"

"Good! So, you can feel it!" She dried her hand, then she said, "Songmi-ya, I want to take this mouse."

"Why?"

"It is a nice fat mouse, and it ate so much food. My children would love to eat it."

When her aunt and her family returned, they were on a mission. "Today is the day, let's catch all of the mice," her uncle said. They had seen mice before. That Songmi was bitten changed everything. Aunt Yeonhui was concerned that a mouse might attack one of her own children. They were going to exterminate the mice and clean up everywhere. They moved all the household items out of the way. They had a water tank where they stored water for various daily uses. They dumped the water and set it up as a trap for the mice. Songmi, her aunt and uncle were positioned around the room, ready to chase the mice into the water tank. A mouse came out running. Then another mouse went scurrying by. They caught 12 mice that day.

Her uncle cooked them and together they ate the mice. A few days later, they caught seven more mice. They had another great meal. It had been a long time since they had been able to eat meat. After a few days, there were no more mice.

Songmi said, "Aunt, Uncle, maybe the mice are telling others that this house is too dangerous for them."

IT WASN'T the first time that Songmi ate something a bit different. When Songmi had been homeless with her mom, she ate frogs. One day when Songmi was bored and watching some frogs jump around, she got an idea. "What if I catch some frogs?" With two hands, she would catch them, then throw them down to paralyze them. She was so hungry that she could eat anything.

In all, she caught about 20 frogs. She began targeting the big frogs. She turned the front of her shirt into a little sack to carry the frogs. Triumphantly, she walked back to the area where her mother and others were still sleeping. She began ripping the skin off the frogs. She could see their intestines after she peeled off their skin. She then put the frogs on a long stick so they were hanging. It would be easier for her to carry them to her mom. The frogs seemed to have their hands up to surrender, like a military unit that had given up.

Her mom woke up to a surprising scene.

"Frogs, Mom! I grabbed them with my hands. I was so hungry."

Her mom started laughing. She was bragging to others, "Look at what my daughter did! She grabbed the frogs and made this. She's like a barbaric hunter. She even peeled the skin off the frogs."

Songmi was the heroine. She did the same thing the next day. Songmi was learning that she needed to do something and not just wait for others.

EVERY MORNING, Aunt Yeonhui gave her husband one egg inside a bowl of rice. Songmi really wanted to eat, but she knew that her aunt always counted the number of eggs in the kitchen. It was food in a picture for Songmi.

Aunt Yeonhui had five chickens. She would check how many eggs were inside the chickens. She would stick her index and middle fingers inside each chicken, then move her fingers around to see when the eggs were likely to be laid. "Oh, these should be coming out tomorrow."

She asked Songmi to do the same thing. "Songmi-ya, can you go check how many eggs are about to be laid?"

Songmi froze with a look of horror on face. "Will my fingers smell?"

"No," her aunt said. "They won't smell."

Songmi started first by chasing the chickens. Of course, they all took off running in five different directions at the same time, squawking like it was the end of the world. Songmi got tired of chasing them, then she used her brain. She put some corn on the ground, and the chickens walked slowly to her, suspiciously eying her. One chicken would eat a piece of corn, then look at her, then eat another, clucking each time. Songmi slowly reached for a chicken, grabbed it by the neck, then put her index and middle fingers inside the chicken. She moved her fingers a little, but she wasn't sure what she was doing.

"How can I check it, Aunt?"

"You can feel something stiff in there. How many stiff and soft things are there?"

Songmi checked each chicken. Only one chicken was ready to lay an egg.

"Okay, where is the stiff egg?" her aunt asked.

"It is at the front," Songmi said.

"I guess that egg will come at 2 p.m."

Songmi wondered, "How can she know that kind of thing?"

From then on, Songmi often checked how many eggs were in the chickens. But one time, she was curious about the taste of the eggs. When a chicken laid an egg, Songmi felt that the egg was still warm. Using chopsticks, she broke the raw egg, then ate it. It tasted kind of gross—she felt like she wanted to throw up.

Sometimes her aunt would boil many eggs but not

share them with her. Songmi wished that she could eat eggs. One of her friends often said she wanted to eat so many eggs that she could start to smell chicken poop. Songmi thought that if she ever escaped from North Korea not only could she see her mother, but she would also eat 30 eggs.

14

STARVING UNCLE

When Songmi was homeless, she knew several homeless people who starved or froze to death at the train station. Living in the countryside, she occasionally saw people who had died in the streets. The adults around her would talk about who had starved, frozen to death, or committed suicide.

Songmi's mother had two brothers. Geumhyuk died when he was hit by a train. From what Songmi heard, people believe that he committed suicide by jumping in front of the train. Her mother's other brother was Geumcheol, who had been an alcoholic who had sold everything in Songmi's parents' home. He was nicknamed "Bull" because of his huge eyes. He was about 5'11" and tall like everyone in the family except for Songmi's mother.

Songmi had one good memory of her uncle. He would wake up at 5 a.m. to walk to the mountain. He would take a big handcart to bring back wood. It would take three hours to walk there, then he would search for an hour or more, then it would take at least five hours to go back home.

One morning, Aunt Seonhui woke up Songmi to have her join her uncle. Breakfast was just a little bit of rice. When they arrived at the mountain, Uncle Geumcheol told Songmi, "Stay here. Just watch the handcart. You can sleep here, but don't let anyone steal the handcart or our lunch." Tired, hungry, and dizzy, she fell asleep on the handcart.

"Songmi-ya! Songmi-ya! Little one, be careful, the wood will be coming down in your direction! Move out of the way!" The wood came tumbling down to her, with Uncle Geumcheol running after it. He organized it and loaded the wood onto the handcart as Songmi waited for lunch.

"Uncle, when can we have lunch? I was waiting for you. I'm so hungry."

"Songmi-ya, you should wait, I'm the one doing the work!"

"Uncle, it is also tiring to wait for someone."

"Okay, okay," he said, smiling. He was missing his two front teeth. "Then let's eat."

It was rice, and the only side dish was soybean sauce.

"Are you ready? Then let's go!" Uncle Geumcheol pulled the handcart loaded up with wood. Songmi was trying to push, but it was up to Uncle Geumcheol. He struggled with controlling the handcart when they were going down the mountain. Sometimes some other people would help them push the cart uphill. Her uncle's reward for pushing the cart uphill was smoking a cigarette. He worked hard like that for several years, but he and his family still struggled financially.

Songmi doesn't know when it happened, but it seemed that he gave up one day. He was scavenging for wood, pulling a heavy handcart for hours, and struggling to feed his family. The whole family got exasperated with him. He was giving up on life, and his family was giving up on him. Uncle Geumcheol was in a downward spiral when a tragedy destroyed his family. He, his wife and her sister tried to make money. After one trip, his wife's sister came back and said, "I lost your daughter."

Uncle Geumcheol and his wife complained at his wife's sister for losing their three-year-old daughter. "We gave you money to take care of our daughter. How could you lose her?" He then turned to his wife: "Because of your sister, we have lost our daughter."

"I'm so sorry," his wife said, "I'm also so angry." There was no way for them to find her. His family was falling apart. He stopped working hard. He became homeless, and his wife often stayed with her sister. She got pregnant again, and they had a baby boy about a year later.

Uncle Geumcheol would visit Aunt Yeonhui's home when he was really hungry, but she wouldn't let her brother sleep there. Sometimes he would barter work for food, but most of the time he was begging for food. Aunt Yeonhui worked hard and had concluded that her brother was lazy. "Please do something, you need to take care of your family. Move your body. Go to the mountain to collect wood."

He would get drunk and slap Aunt Yeonhui even though she often fed him. He would throw things at people. He threw a soup bowl that hit Aunt Yeonhui above her left eyebrow, leaving a scar. Sometimes he beat his wife. He would hit anyone who tried to stop him. The only thing that stopped him from using more violence was that he was getting weaker physically. He had once been handsome, strong, and he had those big eyes that everyone noticed. He was starting to look like a skeleton and his eyes seemed to be even bigger. He was getting more desperate, going to Aunt Yeonhui's home to beg for food. When Songmi was home alone, she would give him some food, but she had to be careful.

Desperate one day, Uncle Geumcheol asked if he could eat the food for the pigs. Aunt Yeonhui said, "No. Then what will the pigs eat?" He turned around and looked at the food for the animals. A few minutes later, he had crawled into the pigsty. They saw that he was eating the small potatoes for the pigs.

"Get out!" Aunt Yeonhui said, "What about our dogs and pigs, what will they eat?"

"Do you think the pigs and dogs are better than I am? Are you only thinking about the animals so you can make money?" He left but returned later to beg for food. During one of his visits, Uncle Geumcheol looked at Songmi with those huge eyes. "If I die, then you will too. The next day, I will come and get you."

Songmi was upset. "Uncle! Never say that kind of thing!"

Uncle Geumcheol was on the verge of death. He walked so slowly. He was whispering. He visited every day begging for food, but for three days, he didn't visit. Aunt Yeonhui sent Songmi to check on him. Songmi found him down the street. He whispered to Songmi that another neighbor had fed him some human food, not animal food, and given him some medicine. Songmi told Aunt Yeonhui that he had eaten. Aunt Yeonhui was getting worried, so she asked Songmi to bring him to the house. Songmi took him some warm soup, rice and side dishes.

But it was too late. He couldn't speak, he could barely breathe, and he couldn't eat. A week later, he died in front of Aunt Yeonhui's home.

15

PUBLIC EXECUTIONS & SELF-CRITICISM

Every Monday evening shortly after 7 p.m., up to about 30 people who lived in Songmi's area gathered together to criticize themselves and each other. They didn't want to do so, but they had no choice. It was a mandatory weekly self-criticism session. They sat in a circle, taking turns criticizing themselves and others. They had to have a pen and paper to take notes. Songmi didn't know how to write so she had to remember what to tell her aunt.

"Who is first?" The area leader would peer around the room.

Nobody wanted to start the session. If they were complimenting each other, then it could have been fun. Who would want to be the first to criticize themselves and others? It didn't feel comfortable, and even the area leader likely did not look forward to it. Everyone was quiet.

"Okay, no one wants to start, so I will choose," the area leader would say almost every week.

The person chosen would first need to criticize him or herself. "Today I was late. So next time I won't be late. Last week, I didn't go to work. This is not good for others because they have to do my work."

After that, the leader reminded the person to be better, then the person who started the criticism session chose the next speaker.

"I am criticizing Eunju because she didn't help others when we were farming. She left home to avoid it. That left more work for the rest of us. So, she needs to change and be more responsible." After getting criticized, then the person criticized had the opportunity to explain him or herself. After that, the person criticized someone else, usually the person who criticized him or her.

Songmi was almost always the youngest at the weekly meetings. She attended in her aunt's place almost every week. She didn't focus on what others said. She had to think about who to criticize. Her aunt didn't attend the weekly meeting, but she got criticized anyway.

"Yeonhui sends this young girl here, what can she understand? She is not even taking notes. How much can she remember? Yeonhui stays home instead of coming here."

"Yes, you criticized my aunt, but she is busy," Songmi would say almost every week. "You said that I didn't take notes. That's true. But I can't write. My memory is good. I can tell her everything. It is easy for me to remember because it is usually the same complaints."

SONGMI'S younger cousin was strapped to her back and her four-year-old cousin was walking alongside her. Her aunt and uncle were out when the area leader knocked on the door to inform them that they needed to come out.

Songmi and her cousins walked about 20 minutes to an area where many others had gathered.

"Children, line up in the front!"

Songmi saw a woman dragged to a tree. She was unable to walk and her whole body seemed to be broken. The guards put something in her mouth so she couldn't scream. Her face was swollen, and her eyes were covered with a blindfold. Her husband and their daughter were ordered to stand nearby. Her daughter was crying, screaming, "Mom! Mom!"

The woman seemed to slightly turn her head in the direction of her daughter, but she was helpless to respond, and she couldn't see anything. Songmi hadn't noticed them earlier, but then she saw three soldiers, probably in their 20s, approach the woman. The soldiers aimed their guns at the woman. Songmi covered the eyes of her young female cousin. In unison, they shot the woman in the neck. A lot of blood came gushing out. The people gasped and covered their mouths to muffle their reactions.

The soldiers aimed their guns again, then shot her in the mid-section. Her body keeled over. The soldiers finished by shooting her knees. Her body fell into the pool of blood, onto the plastic sheet that had been placed underneath her body. The soldiers then neatly wrapped up her body to put it into a car.

Before she was executed, a policeman stepped forward to explain the reason.

"This woman is being executed because she killed another woman. The reason she killed is because of money. She borrowed money. Not 4 million won (3,000 USD), not 400,000 won (300 USD). Only 4,000 won (3 USD). For that small amount, she killed a woman. That's why she is being executed. Many of you are standing here.

If you do something wrong, then you will be the next person to be executed."

The woman who had loaned the executed woman the money had apparently started visiting her every day to ask her to repay the loan. She kept saying that she didn't have the money and, in a rage, killed the woman who had loaned her money and then tried to hide her body by throwing it into the river.

Some children were out playing one day, and they saw a sock in the river. One kid grabbed the sock, but there was a human foot connected to it. They ran home screaming to tell their parents. Their parents reported it to the authorities who began their investigation.

Songmi didn't remember if she had ever seen a public execution before that, but she clearly remembered this one. She didn't question if the woman should have been killed, that was not the issue on her mind. She couldn't understand why the woman's baby and husband were forced to watch. Could children really understand what was happening? It must have been meant to terrify onlookers as well as those related to the person executed.

Some other people around Songmi also questioned why children had to be forced to watch executions, including those of their own parents or relatives. However, no one raised any questions about it publicly.

Wasn't there any concern about her daughter? Songmi could feel anger throughout her body, but she knew she couldn't say anything or the same thing could happen to her. She had already learned in different situations how to hide her true feelings, to have a smile or pleasant look on her face despite the circumstances. Revealing her true feelings could get her into trouble with the government.

People couldn't avoid witnessing such public executions. The area leader would report anyone who didn't show up. In Songmi's case, her mother wasn't in North Korea, which meant she could be considered a traitor and given an extra reason to be suspected.

Songmi couldn't sleep for two weeks after witnessing the execution. She kept seeing it in her mind and nightmares. She heard that soldiers would often drink before performing an execution. Some of them were uncomfortable shooting people. Sometimes they even executed people that they knew. They had no choice but to be part of North Korea's killing machine. Songmi later heard that two of the soldiers were having mental problems, drinking more often, and that one of the soldiers committed suicide.

Songmi later saw another execution. A man was shot to death because he was selling South Korean movies. She learned the lesson that the North Korean regime wanted to teach her and others: don't do illegal things such as killing someone, watching foreign movies, or questioning the government.

As bad as those executions were, the thing that weighed down Songmi the most were self-criticism sessions. The public executions were traumatic, but they were rare. With the self-criticism sessions, she would have to think all week about how to criticize herself and to be ready to criticize others. Her mind was never at ease.

PART II

ESCAPE

16

A BROKER VISITS

When Songmi was young, it was common to hear North Koreans being denounced for attempting to escape the country. But when she was in her teens, she heard some people asking, "Why are we living like this? We thought it was the best country in the world, but now we know that it isn't."

Aunt Seonhui wanted to escape. "I'm so tired of living in North Korea," she said one day. "I'm working so hard every day, but life never gets better. North Korea is not the right country for human beings to live in. I want to follow my sister, but I can't. Because I have three kids, I can't leave them."

Even when people didn't have children, it was difficult to go around the country. People needed permission to be outside of their provinces. Getting out of North Korea was even more difficult. For many people, it seemed easier to fly to the moon by flapping their arms than to escape from North Korea. Even when people realized that North Korea was a terrible country, it was still difficult and dangerous to get out safely. It was escaping into the unknown.

Even though many North Koreans thought or talked about escaping, most didn't attempt it unless they followed a relative, spouse, parent, child, friend, an acquaintance, or colleague.

Songmi often wondered, "Why is my life so difficult?" She envied the children who could go to school and just sit down and learn. In comparison, Songmi was on her feet moving around most of the day collecting wood, farming, taking care of babies, doing housework, washing clothes, and taking care of animals. That was her life. She thought about committing suicide more than once.

She was still a teenager, but she was already emotionally drained. Perhaps the same was true of her relatives: her uncle who gave up by committing suicide when he apparently threw himself in front of a train, the uncle who starved to death after he gave up, her mom and dad who finally fled the country, even her evil stepfather who seemed to give up.

"Could someone please start a war with North Korea?" many people around Songmi would ask. It started to become a common joke, especially when they were out collecting wood or engaging in other hard labor. They were so tired and disgusted, hoping the country would be finished. By "country," it seemed to be clear that they were hoping that the dictator and his family would be wiped out, but they couldn't say it directly. They were sleepwalking through life, trying to survive from day-to-day. Of course, Songmi wanted to live through the destruction of North Korea for one main reason: so she could safely leave the country to search for her mom.

Of course, they all had to be careful when they said such things, it wasn't safe to talk openly about the country being destroyed. They had been taught that even the birds and mice were listening to them.

How could they escape? They didn't live close to the border, so even getting to that point was difficult. The cost of escaping was so high to just get out of North Korea, and where were escapees supposed to go after getting to China, Mongolia, or Russia?

Songmi constantly dreamed about her mother returning to her. Then in 2008, when Songmi was about to turn 15 years old, something she had not imagined happened.

Her mom tried to rescue her from North Korea.

Songmi opened the door one day to see a man about 5'6", razor thin, wearing black pants, and a white T-shirt. Songmi noticed his really small eyes. He looked so nice, neat, and kind of handsome.

Most strangers coming to the door were selling something or looking to barter for or buy food.

He said, "I'm looking for Songmi. Is Songmi here?"

"Yes, I'm Songmi." It was a bit startling to have an adult stranger looking for her.

Aunt Yeonhui came out, "Who is it?"

"Someone came to see me," Songmi said, not sure yet what was going on.

The stranger said to Aunt Yeonhui, "Her mom sent me here." He didn't say where her mom was or where Songmi was to go.

Aunt Yeonhui directed Songmi, "You can go inside."

She had never challenged her aunt and she knew she would have to be very careful about doing so in front of a stranger. This was about her mom! Songmi quietly said, "I want to hear." Her mom was trying to contact her, how could she not listen to what was going on? Her aunt stared at her. Songmi went into the house.

Her aunt and the man stayed outside while Songmi waited inside the house, barely breathing. After a few minutes, the man walked away.

Aunt Yeonhui came inside the house. "Let's talk." She informed Songmi that the man, a broker, wanted to take her to China. She began warning Songmi how dangerous it could be. It wasn't a discussion. She directed Songmi to find the broker near the river. "Tell him that you are not going to follow him."

Songmi walked there in a daze. She had so many thoughts going through her mind. She saw him standing near the river, smoking a long cigarette.

"Excuse me, I was talking to my aunt. She said I cannot follow you. I cannot trust you. She said that China is such a scary place. I have also heard that they sell women to other people."

Songmi was scared by what her aunt had said, but even without hearing her aunt's warnings, she already had her fears. She had been waiting for her mom to return, but she didn't expect that her mother would try to rescue her.

They talked for a few minutes, then he said, "I under-stand." She couldn't contradict her aunt, and he probably knew she didn't have the power to decide on her own with an adult saying no. He gave Songmi his phone number, then told her, "If you change your mind, then give me a call."

As she walked back home, she was excited at the prospect of being together with her mom again. She had dreamed and cried about it for so many years. At last, here was her opportunity.

When Songmi got back to her aunt's home, it was clear that her aunt and uncle were on the defensive. They were warning her that it would be too dangerous, but Songmi could also sense that they needed her. They had made her feel like an unwelcome outsider for so long, and it seemed there were so many times they looked forward to her leaving. She had tried to figure out how to survive in her aunt's home, and she had done so. Songmi had become an important part of their home, doing many things around the house and working hard all day while being quiet and obedient. Even though she still felt like an unwanted guest, she could see that they feared losing her.

Her aunt and uncle told her, "If you go with the broker, he could sell you to a man in China. You won't be able to come back here, and you won't be able to see your mom."

Her aunt may have sensed that Songmi wasn't completely convinced by her arguments. Songmi had never disobeyed her or challenged her, but now her mom was involved.

"Think about it," Aunt Yeonhui said. "We won't be able to protect you, we don't know what would happen to you."

Songmi also knew that she was being watched by the neighbors. Her mom had escaped, so Songmi was deemed at risk of following her. "If the mother is pretty, the daughter is also pretty." *If the mother escapes, the daughter may also escape.* Songmi knew nothing about world geography. She hadn't read or even seen a book in years. She was in the darkness of North Korea, but now there was a green light, possibly shining out a way for her.

Songmi went back to working for her aunt and uncle,

wondering if she would ever see her mother again. But she was happy to know that her mom was still thinking about her and that her mom wanted to be with her.

After the broker left, Songmi's heart was beating so fast. She held her hand over her chest, breathing, thinking, "I have a mom." For so many years, she had not seen or talked with her mom. It was so scary and exciting. She started thinking, "Maybe I can get ready to escape." As much as she may have wanted to escape, she knew that her aunt and uncle were against it. To keep themselves out of trouble, they could report her if they thought she might try to escape.

One day when Songmi was doing some manual labor, she saw some kids playing Red Light, Green Light. Go on green, stop on red. It seemed that everything in her life was a red light. Stop. Don't move. Don't do this. Don't do that. Don't have fun. Work, work, work. There seemed to be only one green light in her life: her mom. She wanted to go to her mom.

Whenever she saw someone standing in front of the house, she wondered, "Is it another broker to take me to Mom?"

In February 2010, after five years of hoping to talk to her mother, Songmi got the chance. She and her aunt went to Hyesan on the border of China to call her mother to ask her to send money.

Songmi cried much of the time she was on the phone with her mother. Her mother told Songmi that she was going to send another broker to rescue her. Aunt Yeonhui was also listening. Aunt Yeonhui had already turned a broker away and warned Songmi about what could happen to her. Songmi reminded her mom to be careful about saying things so directly and that they could get into trouble if anyone was listening. By "anyone," it sounded like North Korean agents, but Songmi really meant Aunt Yeonhui.

Her mother had other questions, such as: "Are you going to school now?"

Aunt Yeonhui had anticipated that Songmi's mother might ask about that. She had instructed Songmi to lie. When she heard that, she gave Songmi a signal with her eyes.

"Yes, I'm going to school."

"Good. Let me talk to your aunt." Songmi's mother thanked Aunt Yeon-hui for sending Songmi to school.

They finished the call. They had to be careful because it wasn't safe to make long international phone calls. Her mom knew she was putting them at risk by calling so she also wanted to be brief.

Aunt Yeonhui asked, "Songmi-ya, if your mom sends a broker, would you follow him?"

Songmi said, "No."

Songmi's mom kept her promise. A second broker knocked on their door. Songmi still hadn't gotten over her fears of escaping into the unknown. Songmi faced the decision again, should she stay in North Korea? She wanted to be with her mom, but what if her aunt and uncle were right? How could she trust the broker? She apologized to him. "I'm so sorry, I can't go with you."

He asked her why not. She said that she didn't want to be sold in China. He explained, "No, no way. Your mom gave me money to take you. I won't sell you."

Although living with her aunt and uncle wasn't satisfying because she couldn't go to school and was working so hard, she at least knew what kind of life she would have with them.

She didn't go with the broker, but she still thought about it. Her aunt went on the offensive, coming up with new arguments. "If you go to China, they will take your organs and sell them. You are going to be like a pig. They will feed you, then they will kill you so they can use you."

That alarmed Songmi. She had been roommates with a pig. She had told the pig that she was so grateful not to be him. "No way. I will wait for Mom here."

17

AWAKENING

The lights were on at the abandoned house down the street from Aunt Yeonhui's home. A bit later, while Songmi was doing housework, a woman came out from the house. Although they had never met, the woman called Songmi by her name.

Songmi was curious how she knew her name. She said that she had learned about Songmi from others when she had asked them how she could make money. Songmi learned that the woman's name was Yeongsil and that she was about 40 years old. The first thing Songmi noticed about her is that she was short and fat. Yeongsil had been away for a decade, so it wasn't easy for her to find work. One way would be to collect wood to sell, so the others had told Yeongsil about Songmi. She asked if she could join Songmi.

"Sure! When do you want to go?" Songmi welcomed having someone join her as she did such hard work; she would not be lonely.

"Right now!" Yeongsil was starving. She needed wood to sell so she could buy some food.

"No way! It is too late."

It was already about 10 a.m. It was going to be about a three-hour walk to get there. It was going to take a few hours to collect tree limbs, have lunch, then they would have a five hour walk to come back. It is a full day of hard work that needs to be started early.

"We will arrive at 1 p.m., so we probably won't get back until 10 p.m."

Yeongsil said, "It doesn't matter. Let's go."

"It matters to me," Songmi said, trying to be polite, but also wanting her neighbor to realize how difficult it was. "That's too late. Let's go tomorrow."

Yeongsil agreed, and she asked what they needed. Songmi had become an expert on collecting wood. She knew they would need the following items:

1. Rope to tie the tree limbs together to make it easier to carry on their backs.
2. A comfortable strap for their shoulders, otherwise, it could be really painful with the weight of the wood on their backs.
3. A hand saw to cut and trim the tree limbs. Songmi was young and not that big. Others who cut down the big, living trees would usually cut the tree limbs off and leave them behind. Songmi and others picked up tree limbs after they had dried and weren't as heavy.
4. Lunch. Yeongsil said, "I don't have any food, that's why I'm going with you!" Songmi said, "Okay, we can share what I have. But it won't be much."

The next morning at 7 a.m., Songmi and Yeongsil were on their way to the mountain to collect tree limbs.

Because her mother had escaped to China, Songmi was fascinated to hear about Yeongsil's experience in China as well as about being in jail in North Korea for a year. Many people had talked about the woman who had been missing for years. Her reputation wasn't good because people knew that she had been in China. Many neighbors didn't want to talk to her because she was being monitored.

Yeongsil escaped from North Korea around 1997 or 1998 because she was starving. She crossed the river around midnight, and she knocked on the door of the first house she saw in China. An elderly woman who answered the door could speak some Korean. She welcomed Yeongsil into her home. She told her to take a shower and left out new clothes for her. The elderly woman was taking care of her like a caring mother. Yeongsil eagerly ate the food the elderly woman gave to her. She stayed there for a few days. The elderly woman was kind, but she also reminded Yeongsil that the police often came checking for North Koreans because they were so close to the border.

Yeongsil found another home where a Chinese couple also welcomed her in. Initially, Yeongsil was relieved to see another North Korean woman there, but the other woman gave her bad news: the Chinese couple wanted to sell them. They were like spiders waiting for North Korean refugee women to get caught in their web.

The couple estimated how much each woman was worth. Yeongsil was older and not as attractive, so they guessed they could get about 750 Yuan (about 118 USD) for her, but about 1,500 Yuan (about 236 USD) for the younger and more beautiful woman.

She was surprised. "They are going to sell us?"

"Yes, they are going to sell us tomorrow morning."

The pretty woman was bought first by an older woman and her son. Yeongsil knew she couldn't fight because they could call the police to have her returned to North Korea.

They asked her why she came to China. She said because she wanted to make money, but that she had planned to return quickly. They told her that she would be able to make money.

About two hours later, a man came alone. Yeongsil was told to get into his car. The man would take her to another place. The car ride took about seven hours through the countryside. Yeongsil had no idea where she was or how she could get back to North Korea.

When they arrived, the driver told her to get out of the car. He told Yeongsil that she would be safe, meaning that she would not be returned to North Korea. Then he left.

The woman and her physically disabled son greeted her, "Welcome to our home." The mother asked her if she knew why she was there.

"I don't know."

"We bought you. You have to live with my son. We want children."

Not ready to accept it, but not sure what her options were, Yeongsil repeated that she didn't know.

"Well, now you know. You don't have a choice. We already gave the money to the brokers." The couple who had welcomed her were brokers and the driver was the deliveryman. Yeongsil had wanted to make money quickly, not to get married. The man was short and had one leg missing. His mother bought a wife because he wasn't considered desirable by Chinese women.

They guessed that she might run away, so they constantly monitored Yeongsil. The mom constantly followed her. They farmed and cooked together. She hid Yeongsil's clothes so she couldn't escape easily. When they went to sleep, the mom locked her inside with her son. Yeongsil felt like she couldn't breathe.

Finally, she had a baby daughter. The mom had finally gotten what she wanted. She softened on Yeongsil, and Yeongsil concluded that this was still better than North Korea. She decided to make this her family. She was getting along with others.

Things changed when another North Korean woman was sent to the area. They got to know each other but had some conflicts. Apparently, that other North Korean woman called the police to report Yeongsil.

"That's why I'm here," Yeongsil told Songmi. She started crying because she really missed her daughter. "What a terrible country," Yeongsil said, telling Songmi about her time in jail after she was returned to North Korea.

"I think I was really stupid," Yeongsil said. "They didn't give us much food, they didn't pay us, but I was still working so hard for them. It seems that I didn't have a brain." If the guards were watching, the prisoners would work hard. When the guards weren't watching then most prisoners slacked off. "In my case, I worked hard all the time, even when they weren't watching. I was stupid."

She didn't understand why they were treated so cruelly that they even gave them broken spoons to use during their meals. "We are humans, not animals."

After Songmi heard her story, she thought about going

to China. Yeongsil had been sold, but she said China was better than North Korea. Songmi thought, "Should I go to China?" If she did, she could see her mother there.

Songmi had turned away the brokers, but now she was thinking more seriously about escaping. Aunt Yeonhui always denounced going to China, warning Songmi that brokers could sell her and slaughter her like a pig by taking her blood and organs.

After hearing from Yeongsil, Songmi's mind began to shift in the direction of *how* she should escape, not if. She would often remember Yeongsil saying, "China was better than North Korea."

China was a richer country. One main thing interested Songmi: food was always available. Delicious meat was always available. Songmi was salivating as she listened to Yeongsil, devouring her words as she talked about juicy Chinese food. Yeongsil was short and fat. Songmi guessed that she might have gained a lot of weight eating delicious Chinese food. Looking at Yeongsil, she said, "Okay, stop. Now I am so hungry."

They arrived at the mountain. They would usually eat after collecting tree limbs. But after hearing about life and food in China, Songmi couldn't wait to eat. The main reason they were there—to collect tree limbs—could wait.

"Let's eat now.'"

Songmi could see that Yeongsil really missed life in China. She asked, "Why don't you go back to China?"

Yeongsil said, "I will." She had to save money first. "I trust you. But, of course, don't tell anyone about my plans."

She worked hard without complaint. A few months later, Yeongsil was gone.

18

FREEDOM MOMENT

A young girl told Songmi that someone at the river was asking for her. Songmi wondered: "Who? Could it be another broker? Could it be Mom?"

The young girl described the person. It was a man, wearing shorts and a T-shirt. It was summertime. Songmi guessed—she hoped—it might be a broker. She was excited, but also nervous about why he hadn't come to her aunt's house. Why was he waiting outside?

Songmi told her aunt, "I'm going to wash our clothes." It was not unusual for Songmi to go down to the river five to ten times a day to collect water for various reasons. Carrying clothes, she looked around for the person. She spotted him standing along the riverbank.

"Excuse me, I'm here," Songmi said. "You came again."

"Long time no see," he said.

"Yes. Why are you waiting for me here instead of my aunt's house?"

He hadn't knocked on the door. The broker knew that her aunt and uncle didn't want her to leave their home.

"Your aunt told me last time that they can't lose you. Think about it. Your Mom is sending her money because of you. You are working so hard for your aunt, so she wants you to stay here."

He asked Songmi if she wanted to follow him. Her mom hadn't given up. This was now the third time that her mom had sent a broker, and the second time this broker had visited.

Songmi thought about it, then said, "I'm so sorry, not today. My aunt doesn't want me to leave. I need to go when no one is expecting it. That means I can't follow you today."

He asked Songmi not to give his second, secret number to her aunt and uncle, saying that she would never get to freedom if she gave them that number. He said that she should call him if she changed her mind, and he could meet her when she was ready.

Everyday Songmi looked at his number, wondering if she should stay or go, and what she would need to do to get prepared. Then one day, she stared at the paper one final time. She held a lighter. She memorized his phone number. Then she burned the paper.

Songmi had rejected three opportunities to escape from North Korea. The first time, her aunt decided for her, but Songmi also knew she wasn't ready to escape then. By the second time, she had learned more and was getting the courage to escape.

Deciding to escape from North Korea was not a decision which affected just one individual. Entire families were affected by it. Some people escaped on their own, unsure which people around them they could trust. Others who stayed behind were fearful that they would get punished for someone else escaping. People who knew about but didn't report others planning to escape would also get punished.

It was February 17, 2011. Songmi had been thinking about her future. For several years, she had been working hard for her aunt and uncle. She had endured many things over the years. She began preparing for a possible escape, including borrowing an ID from a friend. Songmi wasn't in school, and she had moved around so much that she didn't have her own ID. She thought about when she should begin her escape and what would happen to her if she got caught.

It was the day after the birthday of North Korea's second dictator. Her aunt and uncle worked hard that day selling food during the celebrations. Her aunt and uncle were talking about whether or not Songmi would get married soon. However, it didn't seem that they were concerned about what happened to her. They were wondering who would take care of the house if she got married.

The broker had said they didn't care about her. Songmi had thought so too. Now, she had finally heard it from her aunt and uncle. They weren't thinking about her as a family member. She was just a worker for them.

She felt so much anger through her entire body. That was it. After rejecting three invitations from her mom and thinking about it many times, Songmi wanted to leave at that moment. She decided that she was going to get out of that house and out of North Korea so she could find her mom, and herself. Thinking about her life, she saw no future for herself in North Korea.

"If I stay here, nothing will change," Songmi said to herself. "Let's just try. If I die, then it would be better than not trying at all."

Her mom had paid money three different times to rescue her. She had sent money to support Songmi. How much longer should she expect her mother to send money? She wanted to be with her mother, not just have her mother as her financial supporter.

While the rest of the family took a nap, Songmi snuck out. She went to the post office to call the second broker.

"Hi, this is Songmi. I want to go there."

"Are you sure?"

"Please, come right now." She would meet him at the train station. She was being careful with her words, knowing that there were spies everywhere in North Korea.

He arrived after a few hours. Songmi walked around the Shinsang-gu train station, trying not to be noticed. "Is this the right thing to do? What if I get caught? What would happen in China?" Finally, she told herself, "It doesn't matter. Let's just do it."

For so many years, she had been crying and waiting for her mom to return. "Even if the guards beat me and ask me many questions, I would prefer to die." She was ready to leave her aunt and uncle, but she had mixed feelings. On the one hand, she was angry at them for regarding her as little more than a worker. On the other hand, if she got caught and admitted anything then they could end up in prison or get executed.

She was scared but promised herself that, if caught, she would die alone. She had a small knife her mom had given to her. She was prepared to use it rather than remain a slave to the government and her aunt. Songmi's mother may have faced such considerations as she planned her own escape, keeping her plans secret from even her brother, two sisters, and 12-year-old daughter.

Her thoughts were interrupted when the broker came riding up on his motorbike.

Songmi's quest for freedom started at the home of the broker's brother in Hamju City in Hamgyong Province. The next day, she and the broker took a train to Hyesan City in Lyanggang Province to the broker's home.

He warned her, "We can't sit together." His ID was for Hyesan. The ID she had borrowed from a friend was for Shinsang-gu. Having an ID registered for an area is another way that the North Korean regime keeps North Koreans from moving around freely. Songmi would need to explain why she was out of Shinsang-gu and so close to the border. The broker said that if they got investigated, the police would wonder why they were together and where they were going.

"If we get checked, just say you are going by yourself," the broker said. Songmi was sitting away from him. They checked his ID first. There was no problem. Then they came to Songmi to check her ID. Songmi avoided looking in the direction of the broker, she just focused on the guard. It quickly became an interrogation.

"You're a student. But why is your hair so long?" North Korean police were constantly catching students for various dress code and fashion violations.

"I haven't been going to school recently." That excuse wasn't going to work, but that was the only thing Songmi could think of at that moment. She just wanted to get out of the situation and continue to Hyesan.

"Where are you going?"

"I'm going to my grandma's house."

"Why are you going by yourself? Where is your grand-mother's house?"

"Hyesan." She had never been to Hyesan and could not answer any of their specific questions.

North Korea makes its citizens liars to get to freedom. Anyone escaping had to use fake documents, lie when questioned, sneak across the border, and even lie to family and friends about escape plans. Some North Korean defectors feel guilty about leaving without telling anyone, but they know the risk that their plans could be revealed at any time. Songmi could imagine what her mother had to go through when she escaped a few years before

"Take everything out of your pockets," the guard said. Songmi had about seven photos of her mother. Five were of her mom sent from China. Two other photos were of her mother when she was young and had visited Baekdu mountain. She took out the knife and photos.

"That's it?"

"Yes, that's it."

They then searched her body, winter jacket, and pockets. "Why are you taking these photos?"

"Because that's my mom."

"Why are you taking your mom's photos to your grandmother's house?"

"My grandma wanted to see them."

"You can't bring these photos." He took them.

Songmi felt terrible. Those were the only photos she had of her mom. Every day, she would look at the photos. The guards probably tossed them. They could probably recognize that the photos had been taken in China. That could have been another reason they were sure that Songmi was trying to go to China.

"Follow me," he said. He took her to the guard office on the train. There were three guards there.

Standing over her, the guard who had questioned her looked down at Songmi.

Slap!

After she straightened up, he slapped her hard again. Then he slapped her several more times. He was wearing heavy military boots. He kicked her in the stomach. Songmi had never experienced such pain, getting beaten by a grown man. She couldn't breathe, she couldn't fight, she could barely see. She curled up into the fetal position to protect herself. Then he was kicking her everywhere. He questioned her again, berating her at the same time.

"Get out. Don't try to go there. I know you want to go to China. If we meet again, you will go to jail."

At Dancheon Station in the northern part of North Korea, Songmi was taken to the guard office at the station. There were three guards there. The one questioning her was a short, fat, old and strange looking man who seemed to be looking at Songmi in a perverted way.

"Where are you going? How old are you? Where's your home?"

When the other two men went out to smoke, he got more aggressive, first touching and rubbing Songmi's hand. "You are so young." He was leaning over from his seat, trying to unzip her jacket. He began groping her. Songmi looked at the door, it wasn't completely closed. She shouted at him, pushed him with both hands. He fell back in his chair, then his chair fell backward with him in it. She pushed the door open and ran out. She looked back to see that he was chasing her.

"Hey, stop there! Hey!" Unlike the farmer who told her to stop when she was stealing potatoes, she didn't listen. She was looking for anyone who could intervene. She spotted a group of soldiers and joined them out of desperation.

She grabbed the arm of one of the soldiers. She pleaded with him, "Please help me."

The soldier asked her, "Why are you running? Is there something wrong?"

"Yes!" she said, frantic. "He's chasing me, trying to do crazy things!" It would have been too direct for her to say what he had tried to do.

A tall soldier asked the man, "Is there something wrong? Why are you following her?"

He said, "I was trying to help her."

Songmi said, "He's lying." It wasn't easy for a North Korean girl to accuse an adult of lying, but she was not in an ordinary situation.

There were about 20 soldiers there, and several of them were ready to get involved. Outnumbered, the perverted guard left.

Songmi was in a vulnerable position. After asking the broker to start her escape from North Korea, her life had changed so much in one day. She was separated from the broker, far from home, brutally beaten, chased, sexually groped, and she had no money to do anything.

The tall soldier asked Songmi, "How can I help?"

"I need to call someone, but I don't have any money."

The soldier unbuttoned his jacket, reaching into an inner pocket. "Okay, how much do you need?"

"Not much, just enough to make a three-minute call."

He said, "I don't have much money, but I guess this would be enough."

She felt so thankful. She could continue going to her mother. She thanked him so many times.

He said, "I hope you can get home safely." Songmi called the broker. In the back of her mind, Songmi was still thinking about her aunt's warning that she could be sold in China. Even getting out of North Korea seemed to be difficult. She had no thoughts, however, about turning back.

Deciding to escape from North Korea was all-or-nothing for Songmi. Her aunt would not forgive her for leaving and would probably want her to leave the house. Wherever she went, her neighbors would be monitoring her, not only as the child of a runaway but also as an attempted runaway herself. The police would investigate her. She had already been beaten on the train. She had heard about what happened to her dad when he was in prison; she didn't want to imagine what could happen to her.

She and the broker had a new level of seriousness. The incident on the train was a painful warning of how easily they could be separated, how easily she could be beaten or abused, and how easily she could be captured and arrested. One wrong move or one zealous guard could end everything for her. The broker took her to his brother's home. They cut her hair and gave her different clothes. He said that she needed to look different as it would be dangerous if the guards recognized her. Then they went back to Hyesan to re-start the process of escaping.

The broker tried to contact Songmi's mom but she didn't answer or call back. The broker told Songmi that her mother had spent a lot of money already trying to rescue her. She needed to send money so they could start the escape. Because Songmi had rejected three previous rescue attempts, her mom was probably going to be surprised to learn that she was with the broker.

~

AFTER ABOUT A WEEK, Aunt Yeonhui called the broker. "Did you take her?"

"No, I tried, but she never called me."

Her aunt was not happy. She had already been upset when Songmi's mother had mailed a letter from China. Now, it was Songmi's turn to cause her trouble.

"The police are around my house, looking for her. If she calls you, have her call me. The police may go to you next."

The broker said, "No problem."

But it was a big problem. The broker told Songmi, "We have to hide you." He took her to his girlfriend's house. Songmi was again relying on others, at the mercy of the girlfriend of the broker.

Songmi was watching TV at the girlfriend's home when the broker and his girlfriend came back home. As they were setting up something, the broker said, "Songmi-ya, don't tell anyone about what we are doing." She wasn't sure if he was serious or not. He was often smiling and telling jokes.

Songmi was baffled. "What are you doing?"

"We are smoking ice." They had a small plastic bag. Songmi had no idea what he was talking about.

"This is good," he said, talking about the drugs. He snorted something up his nose. "We haven't been able to do this for 12 hours, it feels so good." This was the first time they did drugs in front of Songmi, but it turned out they were doing them very often. Songmi went back to watching TV shows. The broker was showing her more of his life, but Songmi didn't care. Her goal was to get to her mother. Her mom had been in contact with the broker for about three years. Her mother had tried to work with a different broker, but that broker had lied twice about delivering money to them.

He needed money to feed his drug habit, so he wanted to get Songmi on the way to her mother as soon as possible. Finally, her mom called the broker. Her mother sent money to the broker, telling him, "Give money to soldiers for a proper escape."

19

ESCAPE FROM NORTH KOREA

One month after Songmi had called the broker, she was still hiding at his girlfriend's home in Hyesan. The beginning part of the escape had been so chaotic, from getting caught by the railway guards to getting beaten and groped.

Since then, everything had been slow as the season changed from winter to spring. Songmi spent most of the time watching Chinese TV dramas and movies. Many North Koreans watched them illegally, giving them a window to the outside world. North Korean dramas were about fighting for the regime. The Chinese dramas showed people in love and having fun. Songmi enjoyed watching them for weeks.

Songmi was watching a Chinese TV show when the broker visited on March 17. Songmi had gotten used to his sense of humor, but this time there was no smile on his face.

"Songmi-ya," the broker said. "You will be escaping on the 19th. After you escape, you can watch TV all the time."

So that was it. In two days, she would be attempting to

escape from North Korea. He warned Songmi that if she got caught, she couldn't use his name. Being a broker was dangerous business in North Korea because they were working with alleged traitors like her who were trying to leave the country.

He also mentioned the change in seasons as being a danger to their operation. "The main thing I am worried about is the river," he said. Spring was Songmi's favorite season, but the arrival of warmer weather could be a red light stopping her from escaping from North Korea. "I hope the ice will remain frozen, that will make it easier to escape," the broker said. "I hope the weather will be on our side."

"We have no choice," Songmi said. "The ice is melting. We have no control over the weather." The dream of escaping North Korea was now meeting the reality. Fear was circulating throughout her entire body.

She was about to try to escape from North Korea. The guards could be there, ready to shoot her. She could be tortured if she got caught, and her relatives could all be punished for her attempt to escape.

If the mother escapes, the daughter may follow.

It was time for the daughter to follow.

Songmi's mother had escaped but no one in her family had been punished. A second family member escaping could cause trouble for the family. In the 1990s, the government would wipe out entire families. But in 2005, when her mother escaped, and in 2011, when Songmi was preparing to join her, enough people were leaving that the government couldn't kill everybody. Songmi was from a poor family that was barely surviving. Would the regime care about a poor girl leaving the country instead of starving to death inside it?

As Songmi tried to sleep that night, she thought, "What if I stay here? Maybe Mom could send me money to help me survive? That doesn't make sense. If she sends me money, I cannot use that money comfortably. She would be working hard to send me money. I want to be with her, not just supported by her."

Songmi didn't see a future for herself in North Korea. Everything seemed so dark there. She wanted to study. If this had been during the Joseon Dynasty or Korea centuries before, her terrible situation would have been understandable as most people weren't studying during those ancient times. But in these modern times, many North Koreans were studying. It might have been mostly propaganda that they were learning, but at least they were in school. Songmi was doing physical labor every day. When she talked with people her age, they would tell her stories about their school life. She couldn't say anything, because either she had been working hard all day or would need to get back to work. She would avoid situations where she had to write something because she lacked confidence and ability.

She felt like she would have to work hard forever and that her life would never get any better, just trying to survive and barely having enough to eat.

Songmi couldn't find a single reason to stay in North Korea. She didn't have a father, her mother was gone, she wasn't in school, and she was staying with an aunt and uncle who regarded her as nothing more than a worker.

She told herself, "Enough thinking about all of that. Let's just go. If you escape, you can study whatever you want, you won't be starving, you can wear the clothes you want, and you can be with Mom."

THE DAY ARRIVED AT LAST. March 19, 2011.

If there had been a camera on Songmi at that moment, she might have looked normal. The camera would have witnessed her sitting on the couch in the home of the broker's girlfriend, watching Chinese dramas and movies. She was dressed in slacks, a shirt, and the winter jacket she owned would have been nearby. Near the door, the camera would have shown her old casual shoes.

If the camera had zoomed in, it might have noticed that her eyes couldn't focus as she looked at the TV. She wasn't watching what was on TV but just looking at the screen like a zombie. If the camera could have looked inside her heart, it would have seen that she was nervous, scared, and uncomfortable. Songmi was fighting through that fear inside. Would the escape fail or succeed?

The broker came by to ask if she was ready to go. They had to walk for about 15 minutes on the big road near the girlfriend's home. That connected them to a longer road that led to the border. It would take about one hour to walk there. It was getting late, about 9 p.m. They had an appointment at 10 p.m. to meet the soldiers who would escort Songmi across the border into China.

The broker said they needed to catch a ride from a car passing by, but when he said it, he must have known how difficult that would be. They had not seen many cars on the main road, and now they were on a side road leading to the border with China. What if a spy or border guard happened to be passing by or patrolling the road?

The broker took out a pack of cigarettes and started holding them in one hand whenever a car approached. The few cars on the road passed by without even slowing down. Anyone with a car may have been wealthy enough that cigarettes did not attract them.

It was dark and the road was curved. It wasn't easy for them to be seen.

The broker had a flashlight to shine the light on themselves, but it wasn't enough. "This isn't working," the broker said, his voice cracking. They couldn't miss the appointment with the soldiers. He reached into his pocket and pulled out some money. He started holding out Chinese money and cigarettes.

For more than a month, Songmi had been passive, hiding, quiet. The broker said, "You need to help. They might stop for you." The broker held Chinese money and cigarettes, shaking them with his hand. Songmi was also waving her hand, standing in front of the broker.

Finally, one driver slowed down, peering at them, then stopped his car. After all their planning, they had to rely on bribing a stranger to pick them up.

He rolled down his window, "Where are you going?"

The broker didn't answer directly, he said, "We need to go about 10 minutes."

The driver was elderly, wearing a hat, and had a chubby face. The broker handed him some money and a pack of cigarettes. They got into the car with a stranger who didn't know that he was saving Songmi's life. Fear was written all over her face and her heart was pumping so fast. She was on the way to escape from North Korea.

The driver again asked where they were going. Songmi and the broker weren't in a talkative mood. Songmi could barely breathe. She tried to answer but nothing came out of her mouth.

The broker said, "I'm taking my little sister to our mom's house." He was trying to cut off the conversation.

The driver might have guessed what they were doing. They were near the border, they weren't talking much, and they seemed desperate. If he lived in or visited the area, he certainly would have known about escapees and brokers.

They arrived near the Tumen River. The driver said, "Here you are." He could have easily demanded more money or cigarettes from them. Songmi felt so thankful that he didn't ask many questions and didn't demand a bigger bribe.

After they walked a little, the broker said, "Okay, this is it for me. Remember, if anything bad happens, don't say my name." Pointing, he said, "Look over there. You can see two people." They were about 50 meters away.

It wasn't too dark that night because there was a full moon. That meant it would be easy for them to be seen. She saw the silhouettes of the soldiers.

The broker looked even more nervous than before. "I will watch until you get to them," he said. "Good luck. If something bad happens, don't mention my name." His humor was gone.

Songmi walked over to the soldiers who would be escorting her across the river and into China. She couldn't see their faces clearly.

One soldier asked, "Your name is Songmi?"

"Yes."

"Okay, let's hurry. Let's go."

Songmi patted the knife in her right pocket. She didn't want to be tortured by North Korean agents and didn't want to reveal information about others. But she was wondering, "What if I don't slash correctly? And how long would it take before I died from slashing a wrist?"

One of the soldiers reminded her, "If we get caught,

don't admit that you are trying to escape to China. We will say that we don't know you."

Songmi wondered if they were really soldiers. Wasn't the plan for the soldiers to bribe the border guards for a safe escape?

They were with her at that moment, but she also felt so lonely. The broker had helped her for the last month and the soldiers were about to escort her into China, but they were also reminding her not to confess any information about them if she got caught.

They were studying the situation. There were a few houses along the river. About 100 meters away was a guard station. Every 15 minutes, the soldiers on duty were checking the area with their search lights.

Songmi's heart stopped. One huge search light shone on her. Then the lights were on the soldiers. They froze. Two border guards were coming at them with two dogs. Songmi and the soldiers could hear the dogs barking and the border guards shouting. Their voices were getting closer.

The male soldier said, "Let's run. If we stay, they will catch us." They started running, but Songmi was confused. If they were soldiers, then hadn't they bribed the border guards? Songmi realized that the two people who were escorting her across the river were not soldiers. They were smugglers.

Songmi's mother had given the broker money for the border guards to be bribed. The broker must have kept more of the money meant for bribing the guards and paid less for smugglers. That may have been another reason that the broker was so nervous as he said goodbye. He had lied to her, cheated her mom, and made a dangerous escape even more dangerous.

The border guards and dogs were coming at them. Songmi and the two smugglers were running for their lives. Then, Songmi fell. She got up, but then she slipped and fell again, and her body broke through the ice. She tried to grab the ice but it was too slippery.

It felt like 1,000 sharp knives were poking her; but she didn't feel any pain. The two smugglers grabbed her hands and pulled her out. They started running across the ice again.

They made it to the Chinese side, and the guards were still on the North Korea side. After they crossed to the Chinese side, Songmi fell again, but this time there were nails on the ground. Her hands fell on the nails poking up from the ground. She could have been cut badly if she had fallen at a different angle, but it seemed her hands had only grazed the nails.

Then she heard the most awful sound ever.

Tang!

And an echo. One of the border guards had shot at them.

Tang! Tang!

Songmi had heard the sound before at the public executions she had witnessed, but this was different because they were shooting at her. She completely froze as she looked at the nails and heard the gunshots. She could only feel fear.

"Where did they go?" The border guards were shouting.

She was staring at the nails. She was afraid to turn her head in the direction of North Korea. On her left she could see the female smuggler place her index finger over her mouth and motion for Songmi not to move.

Songmi couldn't breathe. It was impossible for her to

move. She couldn't see the male smuggler. Had they shot him? If she moved, they might shoot in her direction. The female smuggler again motioned for Songmi to be silent, again putting her index finger at the tip of her lips. The border guards were looking from the North Korea side of the border, trying to spot them.

At last, the dogs stopped barking. Songmi slowly moved her head to look back at North Korea. She could see the two border guards were walking on the ice. They walked halfway across the river, but they didn't go near the Chinese side. She could see they were hesitating. So maybe they weren't allowed to come to the Chinese side?

The North Korean guards were cursing and threatening to kill them. After about 30 minutes, the North Korean guards finally returned to the guard station.

The female smuggler whispered, "It is still dangerous here. Let's go up the mountain."

She called out to the male smuggler. At last, they heard his voice. "I'm fine." He not only had hidden himself from the North Korean border guards, but also from Songmi and the female smuggler.

They crossed a small street behind the river, then moved up the mountain. The dogs were barking again, so they must have seen or heard them moving. The border guards came back, looking, trying to spot them. Songmi and the two smugglers were sitting down on the mountain where they could see the border guards, but apparently it was like a one-way window.

Songmi was so close to freedom, and yet had been so close to death at the same time. Her journey to reach her mom wasn't over, but she had gotten past one of the biggest barriers, the North Korean border to China. She had felt nothing but fear. She didn't feel cold, even when she fell into the ice. Finally, able to breathe, able to exhale, she felt sharp physical pain. Her hands were wet, but it wasn't with ice or water. In the full moon, she could see that her hands were bleeding. There was no chance to see a doctor because they had to meet the broker on the Chinese side.

They had made it across the river, but they still couldn't feel secure. The border guards could be hiding. There was still much to fear about what would come next. But an incredible thing had happened: Songmi had made it out of North Korea.

March 19, 2011 was the day that Songmi almost died, but she had survived. She could start on the road to a new life with her mother.

20

I'M A LUCKY WOMAN

For the first time in her life, Songmi Han was outside of North Korea. She and the smugglers were hiding from North Korean border guards. They stayed on the mountain for about three hours, waiting, hoping the border guards wouldn't come for them and that the Chinese broker would arrive soon.

It was about 2 a.m. The broker could have been sleeping or helping someone else start on the road to freedom. Songmi was sitting there, on the mountain, leaning against a tree. Her hands were bleeding, but there was nothing she could do about it. Her clothes were wet, her body was shaking, but she didn't feel cold at that moment.

The female smuggler was wearing several layers of clothing. She took off one of her jackets.

"Here, take this."

Songmi was shaking, but she said, "That's okay, you also look cold."

"I do this often. Most people coming to China from North Korea are not fully prepared for the escape."

Songmi's old fear returned to her as she waited for the broker. "Will the broker be a nice person? Will he try to sell me? If others can pay more than Mom did, maybe he will sell me?" Songmi wished she had a phone to call her mom at this important moment.

Finally, the broker arrived. He paid the smugglers, and the smugglers went on their way. Songmi got in the truck along with the broker. He drove for more than an hour and a half. During the drive, she could still see North Korea on the other side. It was pitch black there. In comparison, China was so beautiful, with many colorful lights. It was a happy and sad moment. "Why is my hometown so poor?" Songmi asked herself, feeling deep sadness in her heart. "Why do North Koreans have to live like that? Why are so many children dying with no food?"

Tears were running down Songmi's cheeks as she thought about both her joy and misery. She was so happy to have escaped North Korea and to be seeing a vibrant city in China. Just a few hours before, she had been nervous and afraid, dodging bullets to get out of North Korea. She had escaped from North Korea, but also realized that she could not go back freely to her hometown to see her friends and family.

Her reflections were interrupted by the broker: "Get out of the car," he said in a deep, gruff voice. He was old and he didn't talk much. They walked up a mountain for about 30 minutes without talking. Songmi was wondering where they were headed. She saw graves with oval-shaped tombstones.

"Can I ask something?"

"What?"

"Where are we going?

Not answering her question directly, he said, "We cannot turn on the flashlight. We have to hide." He didn't talk again after that.

He may have gone through this many times. Under a full moon, Songmi was completely at his mercy. He was probably the first person many North Korean escapees met in China. He was humorless and as lifeless as the graves surrounding them.

Songmi was hoping he would say something to help her relax. When she was in North Korea, she trusted the broker because he had been in contact with her mom for a few years. In her head, she started hearing her aunt's warning that she could be sold in China. Plus, she had heard directly from Yeongsil about being sold.

"Should I run away?" Songmi thought, as she got more uneasy. She had no idea where she was. She kept her distance away from the broker in case she had to run.

He didn't ask her to get closer, and he didn't seem to be concerned at all. Songmi stopped walking. She was hoping he might order her to hurry up, but he just kept moving. She started running to catch up with him. About 30 minutes later, she saw a house.

"You see that?" he said, initiating a brief conversation for the first time. "That's where it is."

"Finally, I hope someone else is there," she thought to herself. "If I died or if he killed me, who would know?" She was scared to look at the graves. She couldn't see any other houses. Nothing was around except for that house on the mountain.

He spoke again, "Are you afraid?"

"Yes." She was wondering how he knew. Should anyone be afraid of a rescuer?

He said, "Don't be afraid. There's another woman inside." He opened the door for her. "You can go in."

There was a small room where she saw the other woman. The Chinese broker had been a little late in meeting Songmi and the smugglers because he had brought this other woman to the house first. Finally, Songmi felt safe. From the moment the broker in North Korea had told her, "Songmi, you will escape in two days," she had been scared. But there was one thing that could make her relax.

"Sir," Songmi said. "When can I see my mom? When can I hear my mom's voice?" She felt safer than before, but she was still greatly concerned.

"It's too late tonight," he said. "I can call your mom tomorrow morning. She is sleeping now." There was no way for her to continue the conversation. With that, he left to go to the other room. He didn't act like a hero, but that night he had helped two women during their escape from North Korea. He wasn't friendly, but at least he had not attempted to assault them or take advantage of their weakness.

Songmi started to feel the pain from the injuries she got during her escape. Finally, she could wash her hands. It was so painful, but there was no medicine or bandages. Suddenly, she was terribly hungry. She and the other woman looked around. There was nothing to eat, except for a few slices of bread on the table.

"Sister," Songmi asked. "Are you hungry?"

"Yes," she answered.

"Why didn't you eat that bread? You were already here."

The woman said, "I wanted to eat but that food is not mine. The broker wasn't there, so I couldn't eat it."

The broker was in the other room, but they feared disturbing him. They looked at that bread most of the night, hungry. They were like two hungry dogs looking at a piece of meat. The bread on the table was another picture she couldn't eat. Despite that, Songmi felt like a lucky woman for the first time in her life.

So many times, she had felt sorry for herself. She had hated her childhood, and she couldn't understand why she couldn't go to school or why her father didn't love her. She was often unsure of when she could see her mother again and didn't know why she had to work so hard while her friends could play and go to school.

Speaking with the other North Korean woman made her feel thankful for the good things in her life. Songmi was 17 years old, and the other woman was 21. That beautiful young woman escaping at the same time didn't have any family to help her out of North Korea. She didn't know where she would go in China. She was waiting to be sold to a man.

Songmi felt so grateful to her mom at that moment and missed her more than ever. She had given her a life in North Korea. Now, her mom was in the process of giving her another life out of North Korea. There wasn't much of a difference between Songmi and the woman. Yet, they were starting out of North Korea in very different directions. They exchanged stories, hugged and cried together. The woman, named Myungok, told her, "You are a lucky girl. Your mother escaped and she is now bringing you to her."

After everything Songmi had gone through, it would have been tough to think of herself as being lucky before this moment. She was in the middle of nowhere, hungry, tired, and injured from an escape during which she was shot at, and unsure what would happen next, she indeed did feel lucky. Instead of regretting what she didn't have, she would appreciate the good things that she did have.

The next morning, they had breakfast, but not the bread that they had stared at all night. It was then time for Songmi to meet another broker to continue her journey. She said goodbye to Myungok, and they both cried about their uncertain futures. They were hoping they could meet someday in a better situation, maybe even in freedom.

Songmi was thankful she didn't have to be sold, but she was still being very careful. She said to the broker, "I want to call my mom." She didn't know where they were going to take her.

"Okay," the gruff broker said. He called Songmi's mother.

Songmi could hear music. What was that? It was the first time she heard music through a phone. She couldn't understand the words exactly, but she never forgot the pleasant melody. She had a warm feeling.

She then heard that familiar voice, "Hello?"

"Mom! I'm here! I'm in China!"

"My baby! You were successful! You made it!"

"Mom, I'm ready to see you. I want to see you now!"

"Songmi-ya, I really want to see you. But you will have to do more things."

"What's that? You said you are going to meet me the day after I got to China."

"I'm sorry I told you that. I think we can meet in about six months. Actually, I'm not in China."

Songmi was flabbergasted. "What? Then where are you?"

Her mom's voice was usually energetic. But at this moment, her voice lowered. It was confession time. "I'm in South Korea."

Usually, Songmi's voice was quiet and soft. But in this case, she was the one speaking with energy. "What if I take an airplane? Then could I go to South Korea?" Songmi didn't know there was more to the escape process beyond reaching China.

"That's not possible," her mother said.

"I have already been waiting for so many years. How can I wait six more months?"

"Songmi-ya, you don't have a choice. You escaped from North Korea and you were successful in crossing the river. But don't feel safe yet, you must be careful in China. They could catch you, and you could be sent back to North Korea."

Songmi was disappointed when she realized she couldn't see her mom. She started getting nervous again. Her mother told her that she would be meeting another broker.

"When can I call you again, Mom?"

"You can always ask the broker."

Broker #2 arrived to take Songmi on the next part of her journey. This was the most comfortable part of the escape so far. It wasn't just because he had a nice car. The broker turned on some nice Chinese music. She didn't understand it, but it was more soothing than North Korean music. Almost any kind of music would have been soothing at that point. She was on her way to meet her mom in freedom.

His car had a monitor so she could watch Chinese music videos and animations. Songmi leaned back, listening to music, watching videos and looking at the scenery they were passing by. Just a month before, she had been doing manual labor in poor North Korea, and now she was riding in the backseat of a nice car listening to soothing Chinese music. She was amazed to see so many cars. To herself, Songmi asked, "Are they all working with the government?" In North Korea, it had seemed that only people working with the government had cars.

Unfortunately, because she had rarely ridden in a car, she started feeling dizzy. He spoke to her in Chinese, but she couldn't understand anything. She had one thing on her mind. It was turning out to be a long drive. "How can I explain to him that I need to use the toilet?" She was sitting in the backseat, legs crossed. She then leaned over from the backseat, tapped him on the shoulder, and said, "*Hwa-jang-shil*," the Korean word for toilet.

His eyes got bigger as he was trying to understand. She said it again, with more energy. "*Hwa-jang-shil, hwa-jang-shil.*" She was motioning with her hands and began making swishing sounds.

Finally, he stopped at a rest stop. There was a toilet and some stores where one could buy things. He spoke in Chinese. She had a blank look on her face until he pointed to the restroom.

Songmi was amazed at how clean the toilet was. She didn't know, however, how to flush the toilet. This was the first time for her to use such a toilet. She was looking for a button or something to push or pull. There were no other women to ask. With both hands, she pulled the broker to the toilet. He was about 5'6" and chubby. Songmi was then about 4'9". She shyly pointed at the toilet. When he flushed the toilet, she sneaked a peek so she would know what to do. He then showed her that the button was behind the toilet. She flushed the toilet, beaming as she did it. He laughed for the first time. They had spent many hours together in silence. He was still laughing, talking in Chinese. It seemed that a different person or his funny twin had replaced him while she was in the bathroom.

He bought Songmi some snacks, but at that moment she wasn't comfortable after the long ride. She saw the kind of bread she had stared at all night, but she felt more dizzy than hungry.

After they arrived in a new city that night, Songmi was handed off to broker #3, this time a woman. How many women in those situations have been taken advantage of or even sold?

Songmi sat down on the sofa. Actually, she *sank* into that soft sofa. It seemed that she had been swallowed by it. There are sofas in North Korea, but they weren't anything like this one. The TV was huge and colorful. She had never seen anything like it in North Korea. The whole house was so nice and clean and the refrigerator was huge.

This broker was Chinese, but in basic Korean she asked Songmi, "Are you hungry?" Songmi was hoping to have some soup and rice, but she couldn't be choosy. The broker gave her a banana and some bread. Songmi stared at the banana, wondering what it would taste like.

Alone, she studied the banana. She had never seen one. She bit into it. It was awful. She held it, looking at it, perplexed. "Is this really for humans?" She looked around, wondering what kind of terrible thing the broker had given her. It was so bitter on the outside and yet a little sweet on the inside. In North Korea, people were expected to finish the little food they had but this banana was going to be a challenge.

The broker returned and saw Songmi sitting on the sofa with the uneaten banana and bread. She asked in Korean, "Why aren't you eating?" Songmi again bit into the unpeeled banana. The broker started laughing uncontrollably. "How can you eat an unpeeled banana?" She demonstrated that Songmi needed to peel the banana. It was softer, but it still didn't taste very good to Songmi.

THE NEXT DAY, the female broker said, "Your mom sent some money to buy you some clothes. Let's go to a market."

Songmi's clothing made it easy to identify that she was from North Korea. There was a North Korean embassy nearby; Songmi needed to blend in with the local population. The broker encouraged her to buy more things, but Songmi didn't want to have too much to carry. Her mother had also told her that South Korean clothes were better anyway.

Songmi stayed at the female broker's home one night, then she was transferred to broker #4 in the city of Shenyang. From car to car, home to home, unknown city to unknown city, Songmi was somewhere in China. Unlike North Korea, where it was risky to make phone calls to South Korea, she could call her mom from China.

Every time she was moved to a new broker, she called her mom. She wanted them to know that her mom knew she was with them. This broker already had a mom and her son staying with her, and another man, Mr. Park, joined them later.

The broker took them out walking one night. When Songmi had been in the truck her first night, she was just passing by the bright lights of China. This time, she could walk around freely. Songmi couldn't stop smiling. She was in a new world. It was the opposite of the dark and quiet countryside of North Korea.

"I want to live here!" Songmi exclaimed.

Songmi saw many kinds of fruit for the first time. Then, she saw her new friend: bananas! But she wasn't ready to try again.

She was enjoying this first real taste of freedom. However, Shenyang was dangerous because there were North Korean agents, Chinese police, and even human traffickers lurking about. Plus, there was the North Korean embassy nearby to remind her that she wasn't completely free. She was happy to be out of North Korea, but she still couldn't relax. They only went out once because they had to stay quietly hidden inside to avoid attracting any attention. They stayed in Shenyang for about 10 days. That outing was the highlight of her time there.

Songmi woke up the others one night, screaming. It was after midnight, and she started to wake up when she felt a hand on her arm. She was half asleep and not sure if she was dreaming. She was sleeping on her back. Then she started to feel a hand moving across her body, near her left breast.

She woke up, sat up with a jolt, screaming, "Mommy!" Then everyone woke up, wondering what was going on. Songmi thought the other woman in the group, Ms. Lee, was next to her, but when the hand moved to Songmi's chest, she realized something was wrong. Songmi's face was full of fury, her eyebrows pointed downward as she pointed at the broker with her index finger. "He touched my body."

The broker didn't understand Korean. At that moment, Songmi wished she could say something mean to him in Chinese. Mr. Park could speak some Chinese, so he became the translator. He asked, "Why did you touch Songmi's body?"

The broker responded, "Please don't be angry, I didn't mean anything bad. She looks like my daughter. I wanted to put the blanket on her."

Songmi was furious. She was looking at him out of the corner of her eyes, her brow wrinkled, eyebrows tilted and her cheeks tense. "He touched me!"

Seok, Ms. Lee's son, explained that he had been awake and was ready to pounce on the broker if he did anything. "But fortunately, you woke up," Seok said.

The broker apologized again, but Songmi didn't believe him. She began ignoring him. She would always frown and glare at him.

After a few days, the broker told them his story. He had married a North Korean woman and had a daughter with her. His wife had gone to South Korea. She had promised him that she would call him and bring him to South Korea. He waited 10 years, but she hadn't called. He said that he missed his daughter. He then said again that it was a misunderstanding with Songmi and that he was sorry.

Songmi still didn't feel good and warned him, "Please be careful, I am not a kid."

A few days later, they were waiting for the other team to arrive. Songmi and her team couldn't keep waiting for them. They were losing time and were eager to continue their escape. The broker wanted to wait for the other team because he could make more money with more people escaping together.

"A little more time," the broker said every day. "Let's wait a little more. I heard that two more people should be arriving soon."

They needed to be ready for the escape to Thailand. The broker warned the two men, Mr. Park and Seok, that they needed to look more fashionable because they still looked too North Korean. Seok, 21 years old, dyed his hair bright yellow. His mom had helped him with dying his hair. Using body language, the broker tried to explain what they should do. Seok washed his hair, then he came out of the bathroom. His hair was orange and black in different places. Seok was shaking his head, looking in the mirror. "I don't like it." Both Songmi and Mr. Lee declined to have their hair dyed.

SONGMI FACED several dangerous situations during her two weeks in China. They were stopped by guards on one bus, but without explanation the guards let them go. On another bus, it was the driver who told them that they needed to get off the bus. As they walked around trying to find a different bus, they saw that two guards had gotten on the bus to check for IDs. They hid for about an hour as the broker tried to figure out what to do. A few minutes later, a double-decker bus arrived. They couldn't relax during the bus ride, which lasted a few hours. At last, they made it to a city near Thailand.

"You are lucky," the broker told the team. "You didn't

get caught." It was time for him to say goodbye after being with them for 10 days. They met broker #5 and a new team of nine people who were waiting for them. The next day, when it was getting dark, they boarded a new truck. There were now 13 of them. They were getting closer to freedom.

21

HOW DO WE GET ARRESTED?

The 13 members of the team escaping together were united for the moment, but they had agreed in advance that it would be every man and woman for him or herself if they got caught. They weren't on each other's sides, and the weather and conditions were not either. There were many sudden downpours.

The broker was constantly checking the time. Sometimes they would have to run for 20 minutes. Then take a break. Then run again for 15 minutes. He would give the command, start running, and they would take off following him.

They were pushing through the trees trying to avoid getting scraped. One man fell and started tumbling down the mountain. He grabbed a tree. Others, not so lucky, would roll into a tree. Songmi was running in the middle of the pack. Another person fell and wanted to scream out, but he said "Oops," then covered his mouth.

Songmi fell when she stepped into a waterhole. She could have sprained her left ankle or foot, which would have made the journey much more difficult. The person behind her pulled her up and said, "Let's go." The woman didn't ask her if she was alright; they had to keep moving. They were working together out of survival.

After 20 minutes, the broker said they could take a five-minute break. They were sweating from moving, wet from the sudden showers, dirty from falling on the wet ground, and bruised from getting scratched by tree limbs. Several of them were getting discouraged and exhausted.

"Go ahead without me," became a common statement from three of the people. Their woes ranged from exhaustion to pain to doubt. The other 11, including Songmi, kept charging ahead. They were out of China and getting closer to freedom. They were physically pulling the ones ready to give up. They had started as lone wolves but were coming together as a pack.

When one woman was ready to give up, one of the men asked, "What's inside your bag?" The woman mentioned a few things. He said, "Throw away everything that is not necessary. Food? Just toss it, you can't eat it now. Shampoo? Throw it away, you can get more later. Winter jacket? Do you want to survive? Throw those things away."

Recognizing the situation, the broker didn't ask them to run. But they still needed to hurry. Next, they had to walk fast for 30 minutes. Songmi and her group spent a few hours crossing mountains, briefly passing through Laos. Songmi didn't even know it was another country. Then, they made it to Thailand.

FOR THE FIRST time in a long time, Songmi spoke. Of course, she had to be careful, but she didn't have the same fear that she had when she was in China where North Korean agents or Chinese police were lurking everywhere. Then, it was time to be quiet again.

When they got to the Mekong River, the broker told them that he had finished his job. They would be on their own. A Thai person would take them on a boat across the Mekong River. The final broker sternly warned them they had to be careful and quiet because of alligators. "Don't put your hands in the water. Don't talk. If the alligators hear anyone, you could all die. A few months ago, an alligator ate a North Korean refugee who was trying to escape. So don't fight, just be quiet."

They were even more quiet than they had been in China. There, the police and agents could possibly have mercy on someone. But there was no way an alligator was going to overlook anyone, unless it was eating something or someone else.

Years later, Songmi learned the broker may have lied to them as some people questioned if there were really alligators or crocodiles in the Mekong River. At that time, they were terrified that they could be eaten by an alligator when they were so close to freedom.

The Thai person dropped them off in Thailand at about 3:40 a.m. They didn't know exactly where they were. "We can't move now, it is too early and dark," said one of the men who had emerged as the leader of the group of 13. With nowhere to go, they all laid down on dry land near the river. But no one could sleep. They were exhausted, but also so hungry. One person asked out loud, "Does anyone have any food?"

The woman who had been told to throw away her food said, "Hey! You told me to throw away everything."

"But if you hadn't thrown it away, you might not have made it to this point."

Songmi was hungry but she was too scared to care. She looked up at the stars thinking, "I didn't know how difficult it was going to be to be reunited with Mom."

All the way from North Korea, across China, and briefly through Laos, they had always been with a broker. They had been told by the final broker that they had to find a police station, but they hadn't thought to ask him *how* to get arrested. His job had been to get them to Thailand, and he had done that. Then he was gone. Thirteen North Koreans walking in a group, probably looking desperate and scared, should have been noticeable. For weeks, they had been doing their best to conceal themselves, but now they wanted to be seen. They had to get arrested so they could be sent to freedom in South Korea.

How could they get arrested? North Korea was not a normal country where people planning trips abroad could learn some phrases in the language of their destination countries, connect with people abroad in advance, and get prepared in other ways. How many travelers put "get arrested" on their itinerary? North Koreans need to keep their escape plans a secret, escape into darkness, then travel across countries they had not heard of before arriving.

Brokers could warn them about dangers coming ahead in the next few days or weeks. But when every day was about survival and there was the constant threat of being arrested and repatriated to North Korea, it was difficult to plan for unexpected situations.

There were cars going by, but no one stopped to investigate. Finally, the two men in the group took action and tried to slow down some of the cars. The response? The drivers beeped their horns at them. Desperate, the group decided to block the road with their 13 bodies. One car stopped, and the driver asked something in Thai. One woman in the group could speak some English. She started saying, "Police, police, South Korea, North Korean, South Korea."

The driver took the group to another place. They were using a translation device, but it seemed that the rescuers wanted something else: money. If the North Korean group didn't give them money, then the "rescuers" would call the North Korean embassy. Once the group realized what was going on, they were horrified, but what could they do? Collectively, they paid the Thai blackmailers 1,300 USD. Then finally, they were taken to the police. The police interrogated them individually with an interpreter. The escapees stayed at the police office for three days, then they were taken to jail. They had wanted to get arrested, and their wish had been granted.

At the second jail, the Thai officers confiscated the backpacks and items of the North Korean escapees and gave them orange uniforms to wear. Songmi had a treasured item confiscated from her: the knife that her mother had given to her. They said it was dangerous. Songmi would soon learn that they were right to confiscate all potential weapons from them.

22

EVERY DAY WAS A WAR

They were put in jail for 15 days, mixed in with Thai prisoners. The guards explained to them that they had to follow some rules. The prison leader would give them commands they needed to follow. After that, the prisoners had to manage things on their own.

The first battle they had with the Thai prisoners was over the daily 8 a.m. prayer. This was the first time in Songmi's life that she had heard about God or religion. At 7:30 a.m., they would wake up, clean the room, and get ready to pray before having breakfast. The chicken soup was oily, but Songmi enjoyed it at first. She smiled as she ate. The next morning, it was chicken soup again. Then the next morning, it was chicken soup again. She lost her enthusiasm for chicken soup.

After 15 days, they were moved to another jail in Bangkok where they would stay for about a month. There they met with South Korean embassy officials who inter-rogated them individually to make sure none of them were spies. This was the first time she met South Koreans. She thought their pronunciation was so soft.

The South Korean official interrogating Songmi asked her some basic questions: "Where was your house? Where were you born? What was the address? Where did you live when your mom was not there? When did your mother leave you?"

Nervous and shaking, Songmi answered in detail. She hadn't done anything wrong, but she felt that she had to prove that she wasn't a spy. Her detailed answers did seem to make the South Korean official more sympathetic.

The official searched, but, at first, she couldn't find information about Songmi's mother.

"Can you remember your mom's birthday?"

"May 20, 1970."

The official found the information. Her mother had arrived in South Korea on August 13, 2008. That would mean that she must have spent almost three years in China. Songmi realized that her mother had sent a broker for the first time shortly after she made it to South Korea.

"Okay, you said you didn't study. Can you write anything?"

"I can write Korean, but not exactly correctly."

"You will learn starting now. How about English?"

"I have seen it, and I heard a neighbor sing it. But I never learned English."

"In South Korea, you will have to learn English."

AT LAST, Songmi could be a student. She was 17 years old and had last studied at a school when she was six years old. In Thailand, she started studying English and math.

It was at the jail in Thailand that she first learned the ABCs, basic English, some very simple vocabulary like "TV" "chair" "clock," and how to pronounce words like "fan" and "pan." Then every week they had a test.

There were seven students in her group studying together. Some who had lived in China and gone to school there had very good English and had learned some math. They were split into classes based on their levels. Aside from studying, Songmi hated being in that Thai jail. The jail housed more than 100 North Korean runaways.

Every day was like war. There were many angry arguments and physical fights. There were two shower rooms and two toilets. The North Korean prisoners had to wait a long time for the toilet. People would get frustrated waiting for others to finish taking a shower or using the toilet. Some people who got impatient would wet a towel and wash themselves with it. Songmi didn't want to fight so she would quickly use the toilet or take a shower super-fast. Sometimes when she took a shower, it seemed that the water had barely touched her as she kept thinking about the many impatient people waiting outside the door.

When sleeping, she couldn't turn. She would be squeezed between other people who were usually in a bad mood.

When one group would leave to go to South Korea, then others would pay to get space near the TV. The middle was prime real estate because the toilet could be accessed easily and there was a clear view of the TV. Songmi saw South Korean dramas for the first time. The actors looked so handsome. South Korean actresses were wearing short skirts and dancing in sexy ways that were not allowed on North Korean TV.

The food was usually a lump of rice and oily chicken soup that most of refugees avoided eating. When they were hungry, then they would buy food from Thai people coming to the jail to sell things such as boiled eggs, lettuce, salt, and higher quality rice. They would make kimchi using their hands because they couldn't have knives or other cooking tools in that war zone.

One woman who fought with the jail's leaders attempted to kill herself by swallowing a spoon. She went into shock and the police rushed her to the hospital. She returned one week later, and then went to South Korea the week after that. She was so close to freedom, and yet she attempted suicide. Life went on at the jail, but after that, they were not allowed to even use spoons.

FOR SEVERAL MONTHS after she had begun her escape from North Korea and across China, Songmi had barely talked out of fear of being captured. In Thailand, she didn't fear being repatriated but she remained quiet because of the daily war in jail. She was wary of the other prisoners, but she had no fear of the Thai police. They were almost always smiling. "Why are they smiling so often?" Back in North Korea, the police were usually angry, frowning, punching, fighting, ordering people around, and looking to get money or cigarettes from people.

It was time to meet the South Korean embassy officials. The refugees were allowed to choose which country they wanted to apply to go. Without hesitation, Songmi chose South Korea. She would finally be reunited with her mom.

They were given one week's notice of their departure

from Thailand to South Korea. She had another interview with South Korean embassy officials. They compared her statements with what she had said in initial interviews. She was cleared to leave. Some other people were not allowed to leave because they gave different answers from their original answers. They had tried to hide that they had lived in China for more than 10 years. Many North Korean refugees had learned that the South Korean government wouldn't give them support if they had lived in China for 10 years.

Finally, she could get to freedom and be with her mom. She was so excited, but she did her best to hide it. Songmi had a chance to call her mom.

"Next week, I am going to South Korea. I can see you next week!"

Her mom once again had to give her bad news, "You will have interviews for a few weeks."

"No problem, Mom! I already did the interviews!"

Her mom said that she would have more serious interviews. It would be several more months before Songmi would be free. Songmi was deflated. She was already tired of waiting. It seemed that the closer she got to her mom, the more the meeting date kept getting moved back.

The day before leaving Thailand was exciting. But then they were informed that the next move would be somewhat dangerous. Thailand had a North Korean embassy. North Korea was still lurking even though the North Korean refugees had come so far to get away from it.

The plan was for them to move at night. Their backpacks, clothes and other items were returned to them. They were told that they would have to run a short distance. Run? After evading North Korean border guards, hiding from Chinese police, fighting through the brush in Thailand, fearing crocodiles in the Mekong River, and being in a daily war in a Thai jail, couldn't something be easy as they were about to go to South Korea?

They took a truck to the airport in silence. One South Korean man she had not seen before was at the airport waiting for them. He told them to be quiet. It was dark; they couldn't see where they were. They waited in silence. Then that South Korean man shouted, "Move, move, move!"

None of their movements seemed natural, it was as if they had glue stuck to their shoes. They were trying to move quickly, but it didn't seem to be fast enough. He was shouting at them until they got on the airplane. Songmi was on an airplane for the first time in her life. She didn't know anyone who had ever been on an airplane. Hesitating in her movements, she asked, "Excuse me, can I ask something? Where can I sit?"

A flight attendant told her, "Don't worry, you can sit anywhere."

Songmi looked out the window. "Am I dreaming?" She pinched her own cheek and she felt pain. It wasn't a dream. "Are we really on an airplane?" Songmi still didn't trust her own mind at that moment. "Yes," Songmi said to herself out loud. "I am really going to South Korea. Finally, I will be able to see Mom again."

Songmi was seated next to the window. The 50 people on the plane, with many stories of sorrow, pain, separation, and broken hearts, were probably about to be healed. The plane took off, and Songmi's ears began ringing. She had not known what to expect, but she certainly didn't expect that. "Is there something wrong?" Songmi asked, pinching the ears of the woman next to her, "Are you okay?"

"It isn't just you," she said. "It is everyone. I am sure that's what happens on airplanes."

Songmi could see the beautiful clouds. For the first time in months, she felt free to talk, she started talking to the woman behind her. "I am so excited, finally I can fly to see my mom," Songmi said. "Now it is all coming true."

Her dream was coming true, but the airplane ride was too much for her. She started getting dizzy. Songmi then realized that some people were watching movies on the screens in front of them. She was fumbling around, trying to figure out how to watch. She touched everywhere around the screen. "How can I watch the movie?" She hit one button and the screen turned on, but she couldn't hear anything. "How can I hear the sound?" She had put on the earphones, but still couldn't hear anything.

Finally, someone told her, "Hey! Plug in the earphones!"

Songmi watched the movie, then dozed off. She had no idea how long the flight took.

PART III

SOUTH KOREA

23

ONE OUT OF 2,706

Songmi woke up. The airplane was shaking. There was a voice speaking in a different language on the loudspeaker. Then it quickly switched to a different language. Songmi had no idea what was going on, as she came out of her long nap. The airplane came to a complete stop. Songmi had arrived in South Korea.

There were government agents waiting for them. "Please go this way." They said "please," but clearly there was no choice. "Get on the bus!" That command was clear.

Their first stop in South Korea was at the cafeteria at the National Intelligence Service (NIS) building. Songmi saw many North Koreans there wearing the same yellow uniform. She didn't know it at the time, but the three years that her mom spent trying to rescue her were the years when the most North Korean refugees escaped to South Korea. In 2009, more than 2,900 North Korean refugees made it to South Korea. The next year, it dropped to 2,400.

Songmi was one of the 2,706 North Korean refugees

who made it to South Korea in 2011. She arrived on May 20th, her mother's birthday. The next year, the new dictator of North Korea cracked down on escapees. Only 1,502 North Korean refugees made it to South Korea in 2012. It would have been much more difficult to escape the following year if Songmi had waited another year.

She was a newcomer again, getting stared at by the North Korean refugees who had already previously arrived. The newcomers sat in another room, put their bags down, then lined up to have lunch. It was the first great meal Songmi had been able to have in a long time. There were so many side dishes.

"This is the rice I want." Songmi said with a big smile on her face. The rice she had eaten in the jail in Thailand hadn't tasted good, it was jail food. But in South Korea at the NIS, the rice was fantastic. She was hungry and the food looked so yummy, but she was a bit dizzy so she couldn't eat much. After lunch, she had a health check. She was 17 and shy so she was embarrassed having never gone through this kind of examination before. The NIS agent gave her a cup. Songmi looked at her, not sure what she wanted her to do with it. She told Songmi, "Pee in it."

"Pee?"

"Yes, pee."

Songmi's face turned red. There were others who could hear their conversation. The agent said, "It is okay, this is normal. South Koreans do this."

"But I feel uncomfortable, there are so many people here, and you are talking so loudly," Songmi said, whispering impatiently to her. The agent wasn't about to give up. Songmi tried to evade the urine test, telling the agent that she had already used the bathroom. The agent was ready for this evasion, telling her that if she drank some water that she would be able to pee soon. Recognizing that she wasn't going to win this battle, Songmi went to the bathroom. When she came back, she tried to conceal the cup. She handed it to the agent, hoping that no one would see it.

A few minutes later, someone called out, "Han Song-mi!" It was time for a blood test, and her first time getting one done. When she was in North Korea, she had learned that blood was important. Songmi asked, "Is it okay you took so much blood?" Songmi didn't know her blood type, so she learned that she was O+. Thirty minutes later, they gave the newcomers large name plates.

An NIS agent asked Songmi, "Are you having your period now?" Songmi reached up to cover the agent's mouth. "Please, whisper. So many people here can hear you. In North Korea, we don't talk about this kind of thing."

The agent responded, "It is natural to be on your period. You are not in North Korea anymore. You can be comfortable here." Songmi felt uncomfortable. She could see that things were going to be different in South Korea.

The girl behind Songmi was a skinny 15-year-old. She got a pink nameplate, meaning that she was pregnant. She had been one of Songmi's classmates when they were in jail in Thailand. Songmi learned that the girl had escaped with her 14-year-old sister. The church pastor in China who helped rescue her had gotten her pregnant. Songmi had another reason to be thankful that her mother had arranged her escape.

～

THERE HAD BEEN SO much excitement about arriving in South Korea. After that, the refugees were isolated. Songmi slept alone in a small, bare room. Songmi's mom was right again - she was going to undergo a very serious interrogation. Her mother had told her, "Just tell them the truth. Don't lie. Whatever you remember, just tell them." She had also told Songmi not to be scared, but Songmi couldn't help feeling so nervous. The person who was interviewed before Songmi said it was terrible, that it was much worse than Thailand, and that the NIS agents checked everything.

On May 27, 2011, one week after arriving in South Korea, Songmi was led to the investigation room where a female investigator was waiting for her. She was going to be reunited with her mom, but her introduction to South Korea scared her. She had no expectations when it came to the way she was treated in North Korea because she knew she wasn't important there. She wasn't a spy, but she was starting to feel like she was guilty of something, like she was back at a self-criticism session in North Korea.

The female inspector was nice, and her voice was gentle, but she was strict and watching Songmi closely. She asked her many questions. Songmi could see that the agent was an expert on North Korea. She knew more about North Korea than Songmi did. She had studied it down to the street level. Not only was the agent an expert on North Korea, but she seemed to be an expert on Songmi. She knew everything Songmi had said in Thailand, and she was checking for inconsistencies while probing for new information. "Where was your home? How old are you? Where are the places that you lived?" Every answer had follow-up questions asked from various angles. That first day, she interrogated Songmi for several hours. Songmi got tired and dizzy, but she felt like she couldn't make a single mistake. She had arrived in a free country, but she was exhausted and couldn't relax yet.

"Okay, today you are finished. You will need to stay here for one week. We will give you some paper for you to write more about your life." Songmi wasn't good at writing because she hadn't gone to school to learn it properly. She had learned Korean as it was spoken, not as it was written. This felt like the first big homework assignment of her life.

Dinner time was at 6 p.m., but Songmi wasn't hungry. She did not feel good, and thought, "I am not a spy. I struggled so hard to get here, but I am made to feel like I am a spy." She could understand why such an interrogation was necessary. Still, it felt like a punch to the face.

There wasn't anything in the room. At that moment, Songmi felt more isolated than she had been in North Korea. There was no TV, and she couldn't talk to anyone. As the NIS had probably planned, she could only do one thing: write. When the agent returned the next day she wanted to check what Songmi had done.

"I wrote the whole night," Songmi said.

After reading for a few minutes, the agent asked, "You didn't go to school?"

Songmi said, "I had to work a lot. I had to survive."

The agent had a serious look on her face. She carefully read everything Songmi had written. Songmi waited in silence. The agent asked personal questions, probing deeply. "When did your mother and father separate and divorce? Where was your aunt's house? What is near your aunt's house? Can you describe what was on the left and right of it? Can you talk in detail about the area behind the house? What's the name of the river there?" The questions seemed to be endless.

Songmi had never been on the internet and was amazed when the agent showed her the most incredible thing: Google Earth. "Can you find your house here?" The agent zoomed in.

"Oh my goodness, this is my house." It was amazing, but also unnerving that they could pinpoint her home. Songmi could understand why her mother had told her to tell the truth about everything. They were checking every detail; any lies would eventually be caught.

"You mentioned a place where some blind people worked. Who lived behind that place?"

For the first time, Songmi did not respond immediately. "Why are you asking that?"

"You should answer," the agent said, firmly and flatly.

Songmi described the family of a mom and her son, who she hated. They had always been watching and spying on her, checking what she was doing, where she was going, even what she was eating. Songmi was angry because she suspected they were the ones who informed the police that she had gone missing from her aunt's home. Now she felt like this agent might see her as a spy if she talked about others monitoring her. Songmi remembered what her mom had said. "Just tell the truth." Songmi had nothing to hide.

Songmi was another step closer to being reunited with her mom. Not everyone got through the investigation as smoothly as she had. Another lady had to take a polygraph test and met with investigators for more than two weeks. One man was there for a month. Everything was serious at NIS. Every day had been like a war at the jail in Thailand, but there were no fights at NIS. The mood was so serious when dealing with the tall agents dressed in black and armed with guns.

Freed from their questions, Songmi had a new issue. She was gaining weight. She weighed 85 pounds when she escaped. She was always working so she hadn't known what it was like to be overweight. But at the NIS, she was sitting around. She did one main thing: eat. She gained more than 20 pounds during her time there. Many North Koreans gained a lot of weight during their stay at the NIS. The NIS had a solution.

"Look at you guys!" said the exercise leader. Pointing at Songmi, he said "You are too short and fat, you look like a soccer ball. If I kick you down the street, you would roll like a ball." It was more comedy than insults. It seemed he would have talked that way even if his own mother made the mistake of going to his workout. "Everybody! On your backs! Time to do some sit-ups!" Songmi tried, but she couldn't even do one. They spent a lot of time on the treadmill. Some wanted to hate the exercise leader, but they were laughing so much.

IT WAS late June or early July, 2011. Songmi wiped the sleepiness out of her eyes. Then she remembered that this would be her last day at NIS. In her group of about 50, a few weren't able to leave then because they had lied about various things. The rest of them were happy to say goodbye to the NIS and to the exercise leader, too.

24

HANAWON

On June 7, 1999, the Hanawon Resettlement Center was established by the South Korean government to help prepare North Korean refugees for life in South Korea. Twelve years later, in June 2011, Songmi was one of about 100 North Korean refugees who boarded buses to enter the Hanawon facility. One thought was going through her mind, "I can be free! I can see Mom."

On the trip to Hanawon, Songmi saw similarities and differences between North and South Korea. In North Korea, there would be many people farming by hand and engaging in manual labor. There would usually be huts or small containers for farmers to live. In South Korea, very few people worked as farmers. Machines, not people, fertilized the land. She didn't know what they were at the time, but the greenhouses caught her eye as well.

The buses pulled into Hanawon. This was going to be her home for about three months. It looked like a small town. Songmi, with her bag strapped over her shoulder, got off the bus. After eating, they were issued clothing, a pillow, blanket, and toiletries. They reported to their assigned rooms. They were divided up, with adolescents like Songmi being directed to the student area. The next day, they started school.

For the most part, Songmi enjoyed the experience of being at Hanawon. One, she could finally study. She had not been a student since she was six years old. Two, the teachers were strict and responsible. At first, she was intimidated by them, especially the tall ones. But later she really appreciated that they had a no-excuses approach to teaching them. She learned mathematics beyond basic multiplication for the first time.

Songmi had mixed feelings about starting to study. On the one hand, she was ready for it, almost skipping to her first class. Songmi's group had 13 students in it, eight females and five males. For better or for worse, they would be together for the next three months, taking classes on a variety of subjects.

Her first class was about learning how to use a computer. Songmi sat down in the middle of the room. "Okay, guys, turn on your computers," the teacher said. Songmi looked at her computer, staring at the screen. At NIS, the agents used pen and paper to take notes, and Songmi had written her story on paper. She had seen computers for the first time in NIS as they searched for her address and showed her Google Earth. This was her first time using a computer. Some students had already turned on their computers, waiting for them to finish booting up.

Tap, tap, tap sounds were starting to fill up the room as most of the students were already opening applications and trying to figure out what was possible. Some had already started playing games. If Songmi had been in a foot race, the gun would have gone off, and the others would have started running. Songmi would have still been at the starting line, frozen like a statue. She was looking at the computer, looking around the screen, at the computer tower under the table, the mouse. She didn't know what the different parts did or even how to start the computer. She saw some of the other students were moving their computer mouse around. She touched it see if that was the way to start up the computer. Finally, she gave up. With a frustrated look on her face, she raised her right hand. "How do I turn on the computer?"

"Can someone help Songmi?" The teacher asked it with some amusement. One of the students walked over to Songmi and pushed a button on the computer tower that was under the table. The student explained that the blue light meant that the computer had started. The teacher was talking but Songmi couldn't understand what he was talking about. It was the beginning of her being befuddled during the weekly computer class.

The teachers warned the young refugees that they needed to learn so they could compete with South Korean students. "When you guys leave Hanawon, you will need to know how to use a computer, and you will have to learn to type fast." Songmi was pecking at the computer, typing with one finger on each hand. The teacher then introduced a useful feature of computers. "You are all going different ways, but you will all be able to contact each other through email." Songmi created her first email account, songmi0927@gmail.com. She used that email address for several years.

~

"THERE ARE many foreign languages that are used in South Korea, so you need to study hard," the English teacher told the class. Of the 13 students, almost half of them had studied English in North Korea or China. Songmi didn't even know the ABCs. The teacher would turn on an English song, then ask them to take dictation. Two students who had studied English in China could catch most of it. In contrast, Songmi's paper was blank. The teacher asked, "How is that possible?"

"How can I write anything?" Songmi asked. "I don't know English. I never had a chance to learn."

The students were at different levels of English. The teacher taught the lower-level students the rest of the ABCs and basic pronunciation, starting with the Ch-sound. That was for one month, then the teacher turned on the music again. This time, Songmi's paper wasn't completely blank. "Finally, you can write something. It isn't exactly right, but it is an improvement," the teacher said, complimenting Songmi. She began sitting in the front row to make sure she could hear everything the teacher said. Songmi studied English hard every night. She wasn't interested in playing games. She wanted to learn English. Wednesday was her night to use the computer at her shared dorm room. They also learned English from volunteers visiting the Hanawon.

Two of Songmi's classmates also had not gone to school in North Korea. After a few days, the teacher informed Songmi, three other girls and one boy, "Hey, from today you will have a different teacher and class." They all knew it was because they didn't know math or English. Even out of those students, Songmi and the boy were probably the worst students.

For years, Songmi had wanted to go to school, and her

lack of education was revealed as they learned English, Science, Math, Korean, History, or Social Studies. The Social Studies teacher was so strict. "Listen up, each wrong answer will result in one strike against your calves."

"No! Hey!"

"Uh-huh! Then do your best," the teacher said, smiling. The students called him four eyes not only because he was wearing glasses but also because it seemed that he could see everything. The students weren't afraid. Could someone with such a wonderful smile really punish them? They took the test, wondering if he was serious. The next day, they returned to class.

"Everyone, I checked your answers. Time for punishment for wrong answers. How many answers do you think you got wrong?" He was smiling, so they still couldn't be sure if he was serious. "Okay," the teacher said to the first student. "Jin, you got three answers wrong. Come here. Roll up your pants." He was always smiling, even at that moment.

Jin was sitting in the middle of the class of 13 students. She smiled as she walked up to him. "Turn around, roll up your pants." She turned to face the class. The teacher stood on her side. Then, *whack*! He swung a stick to hit her calves. Songmi's eyes got big. She wondered how many answers she had gotten wrong. Jin didn't scream, but she tightened up, her hands in a fist, her whole body shrunk as she hunched over. *Whack!* She tightened even more. He had not been joking. *Whack!*

Looking at the next paper, the teacher wasn't just smiling. He was laughing out loud as he held the test paper up. "Haha! This student has 15 answers wrong. Guess who it is! This is not my fault. I told you that you would get hit if you get the answers wrong. Fifteen wrong means you didn't study hard." The teachers at Hanawon constantly wanted them to celebrate their successes and to take responsibility for their failures. "Uhm," he said. "Are you ready?" He started making funny sounds, then he dramatically pointed his index finger at a young boy.

"Me? Oh no."

"Yes, that's you. Come on, that's you. Come on." He was beckoning him with the stick, repeatedly pointing it downward. The boy came to the front and the teacher told him to turn around. The boy put his head down; the teacher told him to lift his head. When he did, the boy had a big smile on his face. "Roll up your pants." He did, with a big smile on his face. He was looking around the room. *Whack!* "Oh! Teacher!" he said.

"Are you in pain?" *Whack!* The boy was still smiling, but his body was not relaxed. The teacher was still smiling. "Do you want to do this quickly or slowly?"

"Quickly, teacher!" *Whack! Whack! Whack!* The students were counting along with each swat. Then finally, all 15. His calves were red, and he was in pain. The teacher didn't hit the girls hard, but he hit the boys hard. He was the only teacher that punished them. A few other students got punished. Then, "Han Songmi! It's your turn."

Songmi wanted to run away. She felt shy and was worried about the pain. Songmi walked to the front of the class. She was wearing a uniform issued by the Hanawon. "You got 11 answers wrong," the teacher said.

"No, that wasn't me."

"Yes, it was you." He was looking at Songmi over his glasses, with his head tilted to the side. "Ready?"

Three of the pops hurt and the other eight were

gentle. Then he was finished with everyone. "Okay, now all of you know my style. Study hard. Tomorrow we will have a test again and there will be punishment again for wrong answers."

It was Songmi's introduction to the South Korean education system. She had barely gone to school when she was in North Korea. Now she was in a class far behind even her North Korean peers. What would happen to her when she started studying with South Koreans?

"What should I do? How can I study?" Songmi was really stressed during her time at the Hanawon.

THE DAY at the Hanawon usually started at 7 a.m. Around 7:30 a.m., they would sing the Korean national anthem. Students had breakfast from 8 to 9 a.m. Then they would go to school from 9 a.m. to 4 p.m. They would be free the rest of the day to play, study, or do whatever they wanted. From 6 to 8 p.m., it was dinner time, and then they would be free until bed-check at 9 p.m. They would stand in front of the door, waiting for the officers to do their final check. The officer had a gun at her hip, but she wasn't scary. Songmi and the other refugees thought she was beautiful. They would tell her that and she would smile. She was usually not smiling, but when she came to their room, she would speak nicely. Still, she had a job to do. "Be quiet. You guys must sleep."

Songmi usually shared the dorm room with three or four other North Korean refugees. There were some problems, such as some stealing, while others were messy. Songmi didn't talk much. She did everything she was supposed to do. After about 15 days, they started having some disputes. The others weren't cleaning. Songmi told one of the other students who was leaving the room, gentling complaining, "Hey, you need to clean your bed. I was cleaning up for everyone. From today on, we should take turns. Each person will be responsible for cleaning on different days."

There were other problems as well. One day, one of the roommates asked, "Who stole my money?" They began their internal investigation. They guessed that one of the roommates, a 15-year-old girl, had taken it when she was alone in the room. Confronted, she confessed and returned the money.

Then it was Songmi's turn to be robbed of about 30,000 won (about 25 USD). Every month, the Hanawon gave the refugees pocket money to buy things such as ramen or squid at the center's store. One day, Songmi wanted to go to the shop to buy something. She checked her locker, which was unlocked. There was no money. Songmi immediately thought about the 15-year-old who had stolen from the others and confronted her directly. At first the girl denied it, but eventually she admitted that she had stolen it. She had already used some of the money, so Songmi told her to pay her back later. The roommates agreed that the thief had to leave their room. They told the teacher what had happened. He warned her not to do it again and that she would be in big trouble if she did.

A few days later, she stole money from someone in another room. Everyone in the Hanawon knew her as a thief. She finally stopped stealing after she got into a really big fight.

This was not North Korea. Stealing was common where Songmi had grown up in North Korea where people would steal food to survive. But this was South Korea.

It was the summer of 2011. Songmi and her mother had become phone buddies. She called her mother almost every day from Hanawon. She would hear that same music she had heard through the phone before. She learned that it was a South Korean music group, Girls' Generation.

Songmi called one day. Her mother quickly answered the phone. "Mom, why did you answer so quickly?"

"Because you called me!"

"But I want to hear the music. Mom, next time, let the phone ring a little more, so I can listen."

"You're so funny!" Then one day, her mom called her with some exciting news. "We can come visit you!"

Finally, Songmi could see her mother again.

"What do you want? Is there something you would like to eat? Is there anything I can bring to you?"

"I want a cell phone!"

Her mom said, "You can't have one at the Hanawon. You can get one after you get out."

Songmi was in her room, waiting. Her mother was arriving soon. When the security guard called her room, Songmi finally heard what she had been waiting so long to hear: "Your mom is waiting for you in the meeting room."

"Thank you, Miss!" Songmi ran to the meeting room. After years of being apart, months of waiting, and escaping across countries, Songmi was going to be in the same room with her mother. She wondered what her mom looked like. "Does she look old? Young? Fat?"

Songmi opened the door with a big smile on her face, but also some tears. "Mom!" She hugged her mom with all her might. She was crying, wiping away the tears.

Her mom looked at her. "Oh my God! You're so short. You didn't grow." At that time, Songmi was 4'9". She had expected her mom to be more emotional. Instead, her mom was still her mom, saying exactly what she thought.

"Mom, why are you saying that? We should just be happy to see each other! Do you know why I didn't grow taller? I had to use my back to carry wood. I did that for several years."

They were happy to be together again. The last time they had seen each other was in North Korea in 2005. Songmi had been an 11-year-old child, two days short of her 12th birthday. They were now meeting in South Korea six years later. They had talked on the phone many times, but that was during Songmi's escape. Now they were face-to-face. Songmi knew that her mother said whatever she was thinking and didn't hide her feelings. Songmi had a complex about her height, which her mother would have known if they had been living together. It was a quick realization that they didn't know each other.

It wasn't an insult. Her mom wasn't that tall, she had hoped that Songmi had taken after her other family members in terms of height.

Songmi was elated, but she also had mixed feelings that included both joy and resentment. Songmi had needed her mom, but she hadn't been there for her. She didn't know how Songmi had lived during that time, constantly feeling unstable, and then working extremely hard for several years in her aunt's house.

As they talked, her mother let her know about her guilt of leaving Songmi behind in North Korea. She got angry when she realized that Songmi had not been going to school. Her aunt was collecting money from her mother but had Songmi working rather than going to school.

She could have easily moved on as Songmi's father had done. Instead, she brought Songmi to South Korea even as she struggled with adjusting to South Korea. Her mother told her that China had been the worst experience for her. Every night and day, she drank, regretting that she had left her daughter behind. When she saw a young girl who resembled Songmi, she would run to check if it was her. "Sorry, sorry," she would say. "You look so much like my daughter." She had been hoping that Songmi had escaped to China.

Songmi had constantly been looking for her mom, and had cried often. People would ask, "Why are you always crying? Your mom is not coming back." Songmi would say, "No, I will meet her." For years she had been stubborn, saying with confidence that her mom would come back to her. Six years later, she was standing in front of her, in South Korea. At last, Songmi could hug her mom. Songmi was stubborn like her mom. It was that stubbornness that allowed her to continue believe that she would see her mom one day.

DURING THE THREE months at the Hanawon, the refugees were allowed to go out a few times. One of the teachers announced during a class, "Next week you can go out to learn some things. You can have some real experience in South Korea."

They were all excited and curious to experience South Korea outside of the Hanawon. Each refugee was going to receive the equivalent of 100 USD. For the next couple of days, they talked about what they would buy. "Clothes! Games! Cosmetics!" They were finally able to slip out of the dreaded Hanawon uniforms to wear civilian clothing that had been locked away. The thirteen students in Songmi's group joined up with others to take a bus. Each team had a South Korean teacher or volunteer leading them. They went on a retreat one night, learning from volunteers about South Korean life. They learned games, sang and ate together. It was a fun time with those volunteers and teachers, especially when learning English.

North Korean refugees often seemed to be starting from zero, but Songmi was even behind other refugees. Almost all the other refugees had learned propaganda about the history of the dictators and their families while in North Korean schools. Songmi had not even learned that.

In South Korea, they were all learning about how to take the subway, how to make phone calls from pay phones, and they visited monuments to learn about Korean history. They also learned how to use the bank. In North Korea, Songmi's family members had always kept their money hidden at home. She was surprised to learn that she could use a credit card to make payments. She wondered, "How can I trust how much money is inside the card?" She could only believe the money she could count. She thought banks only printed money. She had never seen an actual bank; she had only seen the word "bank" on money. When she heard that they were going to learn how to use the bank, she wondered to herself, "Are we going to print money?" She went to a bank for the first time during a field trip to Seoul. She went to an ATM. "How can I help you?" was the voice she heard from the machine. Songmi, as well as some of the other refugees, attempted to talk back to the ATM.

For dinner, they went to the 63 Building, a high-rise building in the business district of Seoul. They took the elevator. Wow! It went so fast. They thought the elevator ride would take a long time. They were looking outside, then, swoosh! The doors opened. They couldn't believe an elevator could go so fast.

Songmi and the other refugees were about to encounter something new. The teacher said, "You can eat whatever you want." All-you-can-eat? Buffet? Like the others, Songmi couldn't believe it. Pointing at the food, she asked, "So can I eat that? Can I eat as much as I want?"

"Yes, of course! But don't waste food."

Some really shiny fruit caught Songmi's eye. She grabbed a juicy, delicious-looking apple. The teacher was behind her, "Songmi-ya, that's fake food. I don't know how strong your teeth are, but you shouldn't eat that." It was just decoration. Songmi's face turned red as everyone laughed.

They were loading up their plates with food. Then before finishing one plate of food, some were rushing to try something else. When someone would come with a different kind of food, the others wanted to try that. "See," the teacher said. "That's why I told you not to take too much. This happens every time we come here." So many of them were hiding the food in their bags to give to others at the Hanawon.

After a short time, Songmi was already full. She had

only been eating Korean food at the Hanawon and was still a bit hesitant to try the different kinds of food she saw. There was so much delicious Korean food that she was eager to try first. The teacher wanted them to experiment. "Everyone, be sure to try food from other countries. You can always eat Korean food." The teacher was taking students in small groups to teach them about different kinds of food.

SEPTEMBER 27, 1993 was the day that Songmi came into the world in North Korea. Eighteen years later, she was at the Hanawon in South Korea on her birthday. Songmi's group that had arrived in June was joined by another group that arrived in August. Together, they held a great birthday party for Songmi. It was a Tuesday, six days before she was going to be released into South Korean society. It was a special day in her life. More than 20 students celebrated her birthday that day.

They had snacks and soft drinks but couldn't drink beer. They had fun the whole night singing, dancing and listening to music. Most nights they had to be quiet, but that night, there was no one telling them to be quiet. The officer who would check on them said it was the first time that such a big party was held for students at the Hanawon. For years, no one had celebrated Songmi's birthday. Not only was this her party, but it was the first time for her to have such a big party with friends. They used two different rooms, one for eating snacks and having soft drinks and the other for dancing and singing.

"YOU ARE GOING to be free! What are you going to do?" The students were cheering when they heard this news. At last, they could be reunited with loved ones and start the next chapter of their lives. What did they plan to do? "Travel!" "Play games!" "Go to school!"

"Teacher," Songmi said. "I need to study hard. I know that my mom wants me to study hard and go to a university. I need to graduate. I haven't gone to school since elementary school."

On October 2, they were really busy. They gathered their few possessions, such as blankets and clothes that would fit into one bag. Then they had a final celebration that seemed to be the second part of Songmi's birthday party.

At about 2 a.m., they went to sleep. They woke up late, so they missed the national anthem, but no one was going to lecture them.

Songmi's mom and a social worker arrived shortly after noon. They picked her up and took her to a restaurant. Her mom asked, "What do you want to eat? We can have whatever you want!" She had simple cold noodles.

"Our home is far, so you can sleep," her mom said. Songmi was in the backseat with the social worker. It was a four-hour drive to their destination, Jinju, where her mother lived. Songmi fell asleep in the backseat with the social worker next to her.

25

SOUTH KOREA

Minjoggwa Unmyeong (Nation and Destiny) was a popular drama that was shown on North Korean TV from 1992-2002. Unlike most North Korean dramas, it focused on South Korean life and culture. It was meant to show South Korea as a capitalist country in a negative way, but it opened the eyes of many North Koreans to the affluence of South Korea. They saw people wearing sunglasses, women smoking, and different kinds of food and drinks that North Koreans had never heard of and would never be able to try in North Korea.

Hong Youngja was a glamorous and fashionable character in the drama. She was smoking, drinking wine and coffee, and looked so cool to Songmi and her friends. Many women and children around Songmi wanted to be like Ms. Hong.

In hailing a taxi, Ms. Hong coolly puffed on a cigarette, blew smoke, then waved her index and middle fingers. Songmi and her friends would mimic Ms. Hong's actions. "Taxi!" Songmi waved her two fingers pretending to call a taxi, even though she had never seen one in North Korea's countryside.

Before that drama, Songmi and her friends would copy North Korean soldiers by saluting with all of the fingers on their hands. After that drama, however, they would salute each other with just two fingers. Songmi didn't understand many of the things she saw. She was confused, for example, about why Ms. Hong and some of the other South Korean TV characters were drinking blood.

IN THE BACKSEAT of her mother's car, Songmi was getting a little dizzy. As they pulled into a rest stop, Songmi's mother asked her if she wanted some coffee. Songmi's demeanor changed. "Mom! I don't want to drink blood!" Songmi couldn't figure out why people in South Korea were drinking blood. Everyone in the car laughed, with her mom laughing the loudest and longest of all. As Songmi walked from the bathroom, she thought to herself, "Why are they drinking blood, and why do they want me to drink it?"

After she rejoined them, Songmi saw that her mother had bought snacks and drinks. She saw the black blood her mom was holding in a cup. Horrified, she asked her mother why they were drinking blood.

"Songmi-ya, this is coffee, not blood. This is what people drink after a meal or when they are tired. They drink it to wake themselves up," her mom explained. "This is not blood." The Korean word for blood has a similar pronunciation as the word "coffee." This was

Songmi's introduction to the world of Konglish, a mixture of Korean and English words.

Songmi took a sip of the coffee, an Iced Americano. She spit it out. Her mom said the same thing happened to her when she first tried coffee, but she had grown to love it. Finally, Songmi realized what the people in the North Korean drama had been talking about and what the glamorous Ms. Hong had been drinking.

SONGMI HAS a photographic memory about her life, but her first day of freedom was a blur. She didn't feel very excited because of the long drive to Jinju, and she didn't feel great. She was dizzy and had a little trouble walking on that windy, hot day.

They first went to a social welfare center where she got an ID card. "From now on, you are South Korean, not North Korean. You are free now." Her mom and the social worker beamed, congratulating her.

Songmi started crying. "I am free. I am South Korean. I can do whatever I want. I can study, I can travel." Songmi tried to find the words to express her feeling as she looked at her Korean ID card. It was all so exciting except that she wanted to change the photo. "I look so fat."

The next day, she started going to a Hana Center twice a week to study. Hana Centers were established by the South Korean government to assist North Korean refugees with adjusting to South Korea. Songmi began studying English at the center. On some other days, she joined different social workers and Hana Center teachers on outings to farms.

Songmi was now in freedom. What was one of the first

things she wanted to do? She heard a little voice whispering to her, "Time to eat eggs."

"Mom," Songmi asked. "Can you boil 30 eggs for me?"

Her mom wasn't sure that she had heard her correctly. "Thirty eggs? What do you want to do with 30 eggs?"

"Mom, please!" Songmi said. "That was one of my wishes when I was in North Korea. I want to eat a lot of eggs."

"Couldn't you eat eggs when you were there?"

Songmi told her mom that her aunt put one raw egg in her uncle's rice every morning. She really wanted to eat eggs. She had only tried a raw one.

"An egg is a small thing," her mother said with disgust in her voice. "They should have shared that with you."

"Mom, eggs are cheap are South Korea. But they are expensive in North Korea." Songmi didn't want to explain for long - she wanted the 30 boiled eggs.

"Songmi-ya, the pot can't even hold 30 eggs at one time." Her mom finally agreed. "You can eat twenty first, then after that I can boil ten more." Her mom boiled eggs while Songmi sat on the sofa watching TV. After about 15 minutes, she called out, "Songmi-ya, your eggs are ready."

"YES!" Songmi flew to the kitchen. "Time to eat!" She sat down in the kitchen and peeled the first egg. Her mother was standing next to her, watching, smiling. "This is what I wanted to eat! Mom, you can have some too. This is so good." Songmi turned to look at her.

She was amused by her daughter trying to gobble down as many eggs as possible. She joined her, but after two eggs, she was done. "Songmi-ya, you can finish the rest."

Songmi was eating so fast. She got to egg number seven, then she could start to smell the chicken poop. But she wasn't ready to give up. She had promised that she would eat 30 eggs. Now, here Songmi was with 20 eggs, and she could already smell the chicken poop after only seven eggs. She was determined to eat more. After she slowly finished three more, bringing her to a grand total of 10, she stood up, and walked over to the sofa with the smell of the chicken poop following her. "Mom, I can smell it. I can smell chicken poop. I can't eat anymore."

Her mom burst out laughing. "See, you're not a giant. You can't eat 30 eggs. In North Korea, you didn't have much to eat, so you wanted to eat everything. Here you don't have to worry about having enough food."

SONGMI WAS EXCITED that she was at last back with her mom. She had been waiting for years for this moment. She felt secure being in the same home with her mother. They hadn't seen each other in six years, and they hadn't lived together for two years before that.

Songmi and her mother were sitting on the sofa around 11 p.m. Her mom worked at a market and needed to wake up early the next morning, but she wasn't paying attention to the clock. At times, her mom roared with laughter as they talked that first night. At other times, she was outraged at hearing about the way her sister had treated her daughter. "She lied to me. She told me that you were doing fine, going to school, wearing nice clothes and growing taller." Her mom stopped talking. Then she started crying. She could see how much her daughter had suffered.

Her mother understood that Aunt Yeonhui hadn't told her the truth, but she asked Songmi for the truth about their conversation from February 2010. Songmi had told her that she was going to school. Songmi explained, "Aunt Yeonhui told me to lie to you. She was standing right there when I was talking to you." Songmi apologized but she had still been under her aunt's control then. She could never speak honestly to Aunt Yeonhui.

They were sitting close to each other. After talking a bit more, her mom said, "Okay, that is the past. Now you are free and can do whatever you want. If you want to study or work, I will support you. Now you are in a new world." They decided that Songmi should study first. She went to bed thinking about her future. She had a mom she would be with from for the rest of her life. She closed her eyes and went to sleep with a feeling of security she hadn't experienced in almost a decade.

SONGMI RESTED FOR ONE WEEK, then her mom took charge. She set an appointment for Songmi to start studying to earn the Korean Graduate Equivalency Diploma. She had only completed one year of elementary school in North Korea, and studied at the Hanawon for three months to graduate from elementary school. On December 17, 2011, Songmi started a course to prepare to receive her diploma. She studied from 10 a.m. until 3 or 4 p.m. every day with about 15 South Koreans.

In the GED class, Songmi asked one woman, "What should I call you? It seems that you are a grandmother."

The woman was furious. "What? Don't call me Grandmother!" The lady looked to be about 60 years old. When Songmi expressed confusion about how to address her, she said, "Call me Big Sister."' They were probably four decades apart in age.

Songmi thought to herself, "Wow, it's surprising that South Koreans don't want to be called terms that make them seem old. In North Korea, anyone who looks older than 50 would be called Grandmother or Grandfather." From then on, all South Koreans became a sibling, aunt or uncle to Songmi.

A classmate asked her, "Where are you from?"

"North Korea."

Songmi wasn't the least bit embarrassed when she couldn't answer questions. She reasoned, "I don't know anything. If I hide it, then I won't learn. I have so much to learn. I can just tell people, 'I am from North Korea. I didn't go to school because I had to survive. So please, understand me, I am happy to learn.'"

Her young classmates had many questions. They congratulated Songmi on escaping from North Korea. They asked her so many questions about North Korea and her experience there. There was only one topic she didn't want to discuss: her height. She was constantly hearing, "Wow, you're so short!"

She felt like she had much to learn, but the other students distracted her with all of the questions. She was a bit shy and not used to being at the center of attention. Songmi finally pointed out that she couldn't learn if she was answering questions about North Korea. The teacher agreed and said that it would be better for the other students to ask questions after class. One of the senior citizens in the class agreed. "Let her study."

So study she did. Studying was something new for her, but she did her best, often studying well past midnight. Studying was like eating 30 eggs. When she was in North

Korea, she really wanted to study, but she tasted the reality of it in South Korea. She learned that South Koreans studied English, Math and many other subjects from the age of five or even earlier.

After three months, Songmi earned a middle school diploma. She then earned a high school GED after three months of intensive study.

SONGMI ENJOYED BEING with her mother, but she was adjusting to life and culture in South Korea. Songmi experienced a big change. She stopped going to sleep early. There were so many lights, electricity, and TV was available 24 hours a day. In North Korea, she considered 10 p.m. late as she had to wake up early the next morning to work. Besides, the daily TV and radio programming would end at midnight if the electricity hadn't already. In South Korea, it was possible to stay up all night.

One thing Songmi didn't understand about South Korea was dieting. She had gained weight when she was at Hanawon, but that had seemed to be an issue with North Korean refugees sitting around. Was it possible that South Koreans were trying to lose weight? Being overweight in North Korea meant that a person was healthy and wealthy. She had even seen people interviewed on TV about being overweight. It seemed to be easy to lose weight: Just stop eating. But Songmi realized there were so many delicious kinds of food in South Korea that it was easy to gain weight.

After she got out of the Hanawon, Songmi started calling the others she had met there. She loved her phone. She recorded the things she saw on TV, listened to music, and took photos of everything, even her hand. She had long phone calls with her friends, sometimes for an hour or two. Her mom was amused watching her daughter adjust, but she also put her foot down when it came to her friends. "Don't call North Koreans."

Songmi was baffled. Some of them had escaped together so they had a special connection. But her mother insisted, "Don't hang out with North Koreans. You cannot learn from them. You have to learn new things. They also have to learn new things. It would be better for you to meet South Koreans or people from other countries." Her mother deleted the phone numbers of the North Koreans on Songmi's phone. "You must study hard. You are not a baby. You said you wanted to study. You can be friends with North Koreans later."

Adjusting to South Korea was difficult for Songmi and her friends. Some of them had said that Hanawon was boring and that they felt like prisoners. After they joined South Korean society, however, some of them looked back fondly on their time at the resettlement center. They didn't have to worry about working or earning money, and the people there had taught them about life in South Korea.

Songmi had worked hard in North Korea, but she had never applied for a job. She got her first paid job in South Korea at a restaurant that was behind her mother's home. The owner asked her to do other things in addition to her restaurant duties. Her mother was incredulous when she heard about it. "He wanted me to wash his socks," Songmi told her. "Is every restaurant like this?"

Her mother confronted the restaurant owner. The owner's wife apologized and paid Songmi for her two days of work. What was next? Her mom suggested that she become a nurse. It was a stable job with good pay. Songmi went along with it, but she knew herself. "I don't like to see people hurt and I hate to see blood. How can I be a nurse?" Songmi got accepted into a university, but she worried about studying with South Korean university students. How could she be in the same classroom with them when she had not read a book or held a pen or pencil for so many years?

She had been accepted into a university without going through the same grueling process that South Koreans endured. During an interview with the university, three professors questioned if she could handle the English. "We can accept you, but can you understand English?" South Korean universities were requiring the use of more English in lectures, textbooks, and exams. She only knew the ABCs and a few phrases, such as "hello" and "thank you." She withdrew her application.

She needed English simply to survive in South Korea. There were so many words that South Koreans used that she could not understand. "Mart? What's a mart?" She had no what CGV, a major movie theater chain in South Korea, was. South Koreans would laugh at her when she didn't know basic things, especially words that incorporated English. Sometimes there was confusion because of her accent, but she was never ashamed of that. It was the times she didn't know things because of English words that were difficult for her. Songmi was getting frustrated. She started working instead of going to a university, but she struggled because there were so many things she did not know. She was learning things, such as after working at Burger King she could cook 95 hamburgers in an hour.

Her mother suggested that Songmi study English in Canada. Her mom had a good friend there who could look out for Songmi. Songmi was excited about traveling abroad, but also felt sad. She and her mother had been apart for years, and they were about to be apart again after being together for only one year. Her mother bought a ticket for her to go to Canada. In November 2012, Songmi arrived in New York City, and spent a day in Washington, DC. Then it was on to Canada.

26

CANADA, THE COUNTRY OF FREEDOM

"Hello!"

Two young men, probably in their late 20s, walked past Songmi and her mother's friend Sujin. "How are you doing today?" one of the young men asked, waving his hand in a friendly manner. Their eyes were twinkling. The other young man also waved, although he didn't speak.

Songmi had arrived in Canada three days before. She understood "hello," but nothing else he asked.

The young men walked past the two North Korean refugees sitting together on the grass in the park enjoying the beautiful late afternoon weather. Songmi wanted to go for a walk, and to inhale the beautiful scene. There were families nearby playing with children. The trees were lovely and bright. There was a market nearby. There were a variety of people and dogs going here and there. Some people seemed to know each other, but there were some who seemed to be greeting each other for the first time.

This first taste of Canada was different and interesting.

Songmi had never experienced a setting like this where both families and strangers peacefully enjoyed nature and kindly greeted each other. In North Korea, her life had mostly been about work. Even in South Korea, it would be a bit unusual to say hello to strangers, but now it was happening to her.

Complete strangers were saying hello. Or were they talking to someone else? She looked behind. "Yes, you!" they said, pointing at her.

Her initial thought was, "Why are these strangers talking to me?" She didn't know how to respond and didn't even say hello. She smiled. Although she had learned some English in South Korea, she wasn't prepared for these real-life English encounters. There was a difference between learning English and using it.

It wasn't only those two young men. She saw people kindly greeting each other like old friends. One day, a bus driver said to her, "Hello? How are you?" As she had done in the park with the two young men, she turned to see if the bus driver was saying hello to someone else. She looked at him and said, "Hello." Grinning, he continued talking but she didn't know what he was saying or asking.

Songmi was lost again, unsure what was being said or how to answer. She sat down and watched the driver greet other passengers getting on the bus. She sat by herself. A man who got on the bus greeted the driver, then sat down across from Songmi and smiled. After he sat, their eyes met. He said "Hello." Songmi just smiled. He was saying something in English that she didn't understand. He then began talking to the passenger next to him.

It was a new world for Songmi. "The people here greet each other like friends," she thought. "It feels so good, warm and friendly." For many years, she had worked in solitude. When she had been looking for food or tree limbs in North Korea, the conversation was about survival. Songmi had made up her mind about Toronto. "I want to live here with Mom."

Canada was the most wonderful experience for her. She studied at the Greenwood Secondary School. Her lack of English quickly caught up with her. Songmi couldn't understand what the teacher said, but she guessed that she was asking the students to do something. She looked at what the person behind her was doing, and she turned to the same page in the book. She couldn't speak English, but she could smile and laugh. Her lack of English kept being an embarrassment for her. She had learned that there were these words "Sir" and "Mrs." about the teachers. She seemed to be the student who always got things wrong.

Strike 1: "Teacher!" The other students were laughing. Apparently, it was old-fashioned to say "Teacher." She had everyone's attention as they were waiting for her to say more. But she didn't know how to explain that she needed to go to the toilet. Using body language, she tried to show that she wanted to go to the toilet. She asked, "Can I go to shhhhh?" She did her best to make the toilet sound. Again, the others were laughing. But this time, they came to her rescue, explaining that she could say "washroom" or "restroom" or "toilet."

Strike 2: She still wasn't sure how to refer to the teachers, she was hearing "Sir" or "Miss." So, she said to a male teacher, "Miss, can I..." Others laughed.

Strike 3: So, she was wrong about "Teacher" and "Miss." To a female teacher, Songmi said, "Sir, I have a question." There was laughter all around her again. That teacher explained the basics to Songmi. "You can call a teacher 'Miss' or 'Sir' depending on if it is a man or woman."

Despite those stumbles and many others, Songmi never thought about giving up. One, her mother had sent her to Canada to learn English, so she couldn't give up. Two, despite her mistakes, learning English was exciting. She was able to talk with people from around the world. A third reason she didn't give up: she was too busy. She would wake up and shower at 7:30 a.m., attend school from 8:00 a.m. to 4 p.m., and work at a restaurant from 5 p.m. to midnight.

There was no one stopping her. She was working at a restaurant and making extra money from tips. She noticed that when she smiled and was nice that she got bigger tips. She made enough money that her mom asked if she could send some to North Korea to help Aunt Seonhui escape. Songmi and her mom sent about 1,000 USD each. Aunt Seonhui did not escape, however. With her three kids, it was difficult. After Songmi and her mother escaped, their family members were probably watched more closely.

SONGMI ENCOUNTERED SO many situations in Canada that it seemed she learned something new every day. Songmi thought about settling down in Canada. It was her freedom country where there were so many friendly people. It seemed that she could live and learn without being judged, or at least the judgments might be short-term.

However, her mother told her that it was time to return to Korea. Her purpose in going to Canada had been to learn English, and after 18 months, her English had improved a lot. After Canada, she knew how to address teachers as "Sir" or "Miss."

27

COUNSELING: FINDING MYSELF
AT LAST

Years later, on April 4, 2018, Songmi posted on Instagram: "Now I am zero." Zero had always been her favorite number. "I can make any number with zero. Just add more zeros to any number." But she was also at zero in her life because of several personal problems, feeling like she was starting over again.

Almost two years later, in February 2020, Songmi was asking herself why she was living. She was afraid to open her eyes in the morning, wondering, "Should I commit suicide today?" Nine years to the day after she began her escape from North Korea, she wrote a note on a South Korean messaging board. "I'm afraid of tomorrow. What should I do? I feel like I am losing myself." The cloud of suicide was hanging over her head.

She took a shower with suicide on her mind. Then she saw the tattoo of her son's name above the left side of her chest. When Songmi had been going through a difficult time in 2019, she got the tattoo. Songmi was ready to give up when she went through this difficult time, but then she thought about her son. "Who would care for him if I killed myself? I grew up without a mother. I can't let that happen to my son."

Looking to save herself, she visited a couple of counseling centers for North Korean refugees. Finally, she cried as she talked with the head of one of the centers. They asked her: "Are you ready to accept counseling? What would you like to change through this psychological counseling?"

Songmi wanted three things: "One, I want to find myself, I want to find the real Songmi. Two, I want to have a better relationship with my mom. Three, I want to gain confidence and prepare for my future."

March 1, 2020 was the day Songmi started psychological counseling, but it took some time for her to accept counseling. Initially, there were 10 North Korean refugees, nine of whom were women, in her counseling group. She started by filling out a questionnaire of about 150 questions about family, parents, and childhood. She looked at one of the questions for about three minutes, wondering how she could explain the many things she could feel bubbling up. Finally, she wrote, "I don't know."

She doodled in frustration for about 30 minutes, giving short answers to the questions. The counselor came over to her, "Please, focus on the questions." A few minutes later, tears began rolling down Songmi's cheeks and onto the paper. She had stopped writing, the pen in her hand was frozen by her thoughts. She turned her head and saw several of the other North Korean refugees were also crying.

Songmi started both individual and group sessions. The individual sessions usually lasted an hour, while the group sessions lasted a few hours. Still, she didn't feel comfortable. She wasn't ready to open up yet. She often expressed her frustration at the questions and avoided giving direct explanations. In one of the individual sessions, Songmi and the counselor were seated on sofas across from each other.

The counselor said, "It seems that you are smiling all of the time, right?"

"Yes, I am."

Making eye contact with Songmi, the counselor said, "That means you don't want to show others your real feelings." Songmi didn't respond immediately. She continued smiling, but she had an uncomfortable feeling. Her frustration turned to anger.

The counselor then said point-blank, "That's a fake smile."

Songmi was in denial. "No. Why would I have a fake smile?"

The counselor said, "Because you don't want to show people what is inside. You want to hide what is there. That's not just you. There are many people who want to hide their real feelings."

Songmi leaned over. She was now listening. Curious.

The counselor continued, looking directly at Songmi: "It seems that you are not ready to open up yet." The counselor probably sensed she had made a breakthrough. Like lightning, she struck, then was gone. "Okay, I think we can shift the conversation now. How was last week?" The counselor had completely pivoted away from her challenge. She continued making eye contact. Songmi looked away. The counselor asked Songmi about her son.

"He's fine." Songmi looked around the room with her eyes, but did not make eye contact with the counselor. She answered the counselor's questions, thinking about her life. Walking to the bus station, Songmi's heart felt heavy. She could feel pain inside, and she was having trouble breathing. She began thinking about when she was a child. She felt the tears rolling down her cheeks. She was in public, but she didn't try to hide her feelings. On the bus, she kept thinking. "Am I living with a fake smile? How long have I been like this? Who is the real Songmi?"

As she reflected on her life, Songmi remembered when neighbors in North Korea questioned if her smile was real. In South Korea, she realized they may have been right. She had been living with a fake smile, hiding her pain. She had wanted people to think she was doing as well as other kids.

One of the videos the counselors shared in a group session with the refugees showed North Korean refugee mothers explaining why they had left their children behind in North Korea and China. Songmi thought to herself, "It feels like they are explaining Mom's story to me."

In an individual session with a counselor, Songmi finally admitted some of the things she had been suppressing. She said things she had been unable to say aloud before, what she had tried to block out of her mind behind her fake smile: "Mom gave me my first life when I was born, then she gave me a second life when she brought me to South Korea. But I have some resentment that I haven't been able to express. How could she leave me behind in North Korea without even saying goodbye or explaining she was planning to escape?"

It was the impolite question that she had not been able to ask herself. She had trusted her mother after their time living together in a barn. No matter how many times she had gone looking for her mother, she had been secure in the thought that they would always be together and that she could always find her mother in North Korea anytime she went looking for her. But what then, after her mother left her behind in North Korea?

During the year, Songmi and her mother had some difficult conversations about Songmi's childhood. Her mother explained that she had left Songmi behind because she didn't think it was possible for them to escape together. If they had been captured in China, they would have been separated and Songmi could have been sold. Once her mother was in a stronger position, then she could rescue Songmi.

After counseling and talking more deeply with her mother, she could understand the difficult decision her mother had made. When her counseling ended in early 2021, the head of the center asked her the same questions they had asked when she had cried in front of them. She explained that her relationship with her mother had improved drastically. She was still going to struggle with finding herself and preparing for her future, but she had reunited with the green light of her life and she had become the green light of her son's life. Songmi had opened up. She had found her voice.

AFTERWORD

The best time in my life was during the 18 months that I was in Canada. I was young and learning about the world for the first time. The second-best time in my life is now. I am living only with my son. That means that no one can blame or hurt me. I went through so much in my childhood, waiting for my mom, living in a barn, being homeless, watching my mom get physically abused, having to carry wood on my back and working hard from a young age, then enduring several terrible years in South Korea. It hasn't been easy, but I feel so lucky. My co-author and I considered many different titles for this book. One was "Lucky." I had been through so much, but I felt lucky. Other titles we considered were "Grateful" and Thankfulness."

After escaping, I realized how lucky I am. I saw other children starve to death when I was in North Korea. I had an aunt who allowed me to live with her despite her own struggles to survive. When I was crossing the river from North Korea to China, the border guards shot at us, but their bullets missed us, and we didn't get caught. Many people are killed or die as they try to escape from North Korea, but I lived. I feel lucky to have survived and escaped from North Korea. During my escape, I didn't get sold. I felt lucky because my mom was arranging for me to get to freedom, unlike the beautiful lady that I met my first night in China. Now, when I think back, I realize that I had been lucky so many times. In South Korea, I had some bad things happen to me, but I survived those things too. Now, I am lucky because I have good people around me.

I dedicate this book to my mom because she is the Greenlight of my life. She could have easily forgotten about me or moved on after she escaped. But as soon as she got to South Korea, she prepared to rescue me. I was a child who had spent several years in an unstable situation, working to survive. I can't count how many times I cried when we were apart. I dreamt of being able to hug her one day and to sleep in her arms again.

Now, I am a mom, and I always tell my son, "You are my everything." He is my angel. I had such a happy time being with my mom when I was young, and now I want to have a lifetime of memories with my son. He has no idea what kind of life that I had in North Korea. I want my son to have a happy life, to experience more than I did with my own mom. I want to be the Greenlight of his life, the person that he knows he can always go to for comfort and love.

I spent the first 17 years of my life in North Korea, seven months escaping and waiting to be allowed into South Korean society, and 11 years in South Korea. The biggest difference between North and South Korea? When I do things in South Korea, it is no longer only about survival. Cooking North Korean food reminds me of when I sold food as a child. I used to help my aunt make food, but I couldn't eat it. It was "food in the picture." If I ate any of the food that I cooked, then I could have gotten kicked out of my aunt's home.

Now I cook and eat whatever I want. I can share with others the kind of food that I ate when I was in my hometown. I remember the first time some North Korean refugees asked me to cook for them. I didn't think about them paying me because I was happy that they ate the food that I cooked, which was meaningful to me. Cooking is a hobby for me now, and I am lucky that it is no longer about survival.

I even feel lucky that I am writing a book. If I were not a lucky woman, then none of this would have been possible. I had never thought about telling my story. I felt lucky to have survived, but it seemed that the things that happened to me would be sad for other people to read about. I didn't know that people could be interested in the life of a North Korean who wasn't part of the elite or a celebrity. My life hasn't always been happy.

When I was in North Korea, I never could have written a book. My friends and relatives in North Korea who saw me starving, homeless, searching for my mom and carrying wood on my back would never believe that I could write a book and that people around the world could be interested in reading my story.

After being out of North Korea for 11 years, why am I now writing a book?

When I was in North Korea, I had no voice and no hope. In South Korea, I found myself to be vulnerable.

There are many North Koreans who are as vulnerable as I was, unsure of how to live well. I considered suicide in both countries. People are shocked when they hear about North Korean refugees considering or committing suicide. "She escaped from North Korea! How could she even think about suicide?" I understand the question, but life in South Korea should not be viewed as a snapshot when there is an ongoing movie of their lives. Many North Koreans struggle for basic survival in North Korea, must risk their lives to get to freedom, then when they struggle in South Korea, there is a feeling that yet another terrible thing has happened in their lives.

I was lucky to get out of North Korea, and I feel even more lucky because an amazing person began helping me in South Korea. It started in late 2019 when I began focusing on improving my English. A friend told me about an organization named Teach North Korean Refugees (renamed Freedom Speakers International). I was so amazed as I watched the videos and read articles about the organization. It seemed to be a dream come true.

I learned that the co-founder was an American named Casey Lartigue. I contacted him to ask about applying to the organization as a student. He directed me to the online application process. A few weeks later, I met with him and FSI co-founder Eunkoo Lee. Was there really an organization that focused on helping North Korean refugees? I told them a little about my struggles. After my second visit, Mr. Casey and Ms. Eunkoo had talked about me. Mr. Casey invited me to the most wonderful event. It was the first time in my life that I went to such a grand event. It was a Harvard University alumni event held at the Chosun Hotel in Seoul. The whole night, I felt like I was dreaming. I remember rushing to the hotel.

The night was incredible. I wanted to understand everything being said, but my English was so poor. Even when I understood, I was too nervous and shy to speak. My eyes shone with happiness as I smiled the whole night, unable to hide my feelings. It was an elegant night. We had a fancy dinner. Educated and professional people were drinking and talking about many things, much of which I couldn't understand. Harvard professors and alumni were there. I met Mr. Park Jin, a member of South Korea's National Assembly who was so nice in greeting me. I stopped going to school in North Korea after one year of elementary school. I had never heard of Harvard University.

The most exciting moment of the night was when they had a quiz about Harvard University's history. When the announcer asked a few of the questions, Mr. Casey pointed at me, trying to get the announcer's attention. Then, it happened! The announcer pointed at me. I stood up, excited as a person brought the microphone over to me. Mr. Casey said to me, "Just say 'eight'." I had been shy all night, but not at that moment. Very loudly and proudly, I said, "Eight!"

The announcer said I was right, and I won coffee from Harvard alumni! I was in a room with Harvard professors and alumni, and I was the person with the right answer! The right answer was "eight." Eight what, I didn't know. Mr. Casey later told me that "eight" was the number of Harvard graduates who had become president of the United States. Mr. Casey could have won the coffee, but instead he told me the answer so I could win. It was an amazing night.

Later that night, I sent the photos to Mom. "Mom, I went to this event. It is really special."

She asked, "Why is it special?"

"I met Harvard professors."

She also got excited as she heard more details. Her daughter who hadn't studied or seen a book for years when she was in North Korea was in the same room with Harvard alumni. She said to me, "I think you are a lucky girl to have met Harvard professors. I am so grateful Mr. Casey took you there." Mom is always worried about me. After we reconciled in South Korea, our relationship got even stronger than before. It was a wonderful moment. I was a daughter telling her mom about a special night.

I didn't even know anything about Harvard University when I was in North Korea. I searched online to learn more about Harvard University. I was so excited, telling Mom about Harvard University as if she also had never heard of it.

Mom asked, "Are you crazy? You didn't know about Harvard?"

"Mom," I said. "I had never heard about Harvard when I was in North Korea. I had to work to survive. I feel so lucky."

I finally told Mr. Casey more about the problems I was having. He was disappointed that I had not told him sooner. He said that he would help me organize my life. He truly became an angel looking over me. He has helped many North Korean refugees, I felt lucky that he became my life mentor and my hero. I told him more about my life story. Instead of being sad, he would laugh loudly! That's when he told me that many people would love my stories if I ever wrote a book. Before counseling and reconciling with my mom, I didn't think about talking publicly. My life was settling down, but after he became my life mentor, I could feel that I was ready to speak.

So many bad things have happened to me in my life. After getting over my trauma, learning about the real Songmi, and starting to plan for my future, I felt the courage to tell my story to heal my own heart and hopefully to let people know that there are others quietly suffering. North Korean refugees who are vulnerable can have their lives changed by the good or bad people they meet. Mr. Casey patiently listened to me tell my story even though my English isn't very good. When I got frustrated at not being able to express everything that I wanted, he would praise and encourage me to continue. I could see that he was trying to figure out some of the incorrect English that I had used without mocking me or making me feel inadequate.

I still didn't believe that people would want to read my story, so he said he would run a test. He set up a pre-order campaign inviting people to buy my book in advance. I didn't believe anyone would buy the book in advance, but many people did. At the end of 2021, we already had more than 600 requests for the book. It is hard to express how thankful I am to every person who pre-ordered.

I was amazed that many people bought the book even before they heard details about me. I'm not a celebrity; I'm not on TV; I wasn't rich or part of the elite of North Korea; so, I didn't think anyone would be interested in my story. I was so busy working, caring for my son. I wasn't thinking about my future. I was just thinking about my small family, trying to survive.

As we worked on the book, Mr. Casey asked me what I

thought should be on the cover of the book. I had no idea. He went through my social media, asking me about different photos, then he zeroed in on a photo in which I was holding my face with a forced smile. He said that he had seen me smile so much, but he sensed there was a deeper story behind the photo.

That picture is so meaningful for me. People were telling me that the photo was cute, but when I took it, I was really suffering. During that time, I was thinking to myself, "Don't lose your smile. No matter what, don't let anyone take your smile." I used my fingers to force myself to smile. It wasn't a real smile.

Out of the many bad periods of in my life, that was the worst. I was crying all the time and I couldn't even fake a smile. My friends would take me singing, out to eat, and tried other things to cheer me up. Nothing worked, I couldn't smile.

Using my hands, I placed my fingers on my face. I held my face in the form of a smile. I was asking myself why I was living. I hated being alive. Why was I living like this? Did I do something wrong in a past life? I didn't want to lose my smile. I had struggled with so many things in my life, in both North and South Korea, but I have gotten through them. I had been a playful tomboy when I was a young girl, throwing pillows at my uncle and laughing about everything.

More than two decades later, I can smile. I left North Korea because everything seemed dark. At last, I can see a future for myself. When people ask me how I am doing, I say, "I'm doing great. I'm breathing, I can see, I can hear. I am grateful to be alive. Every moment I feel thankful to be alive and free to do as I want."

I can smile every day and truly mean it.

ACKNOWLEDGMENTS

First, I want to thank the important people and organizations in my life that helped make this book possible. Thank you, Mom. I am here, living in freedom because of you. Thank you for giving me two different lives. Life on this Earth, when you gave birth to me in North Korea. Then you rescued me from North Korea, so I could live in freedom. You also helped me see a different world when you sent me to Canada. I followed you all over North Korea, then I followed you here to South Korea. I hope that I am never far away from you, but, if necessary, I would follow you anywhere because you are at the center of my universe and the Greenlight of my life.

Thank you, son. I hope that I am the Greenlight in your life. You gave me many laughs as I worked on this book, I am thankful that you cheered me up every day. You didn't know that I was writing about some painful times in my life. When I was your age, I was starving in North Korea. I am happy that you were born in South Korea and won't have to escape to freedom.

Thank you forever to my hero Mr. Casey Lartigue Jr., the amazing co-founder of Freedom Speakers International. Without you, this book would not have been possible. You suggested it, then you made it happen. I never considered writing my story, but here is my book. I have been lucky to have several mentors, but you have changed my life. Even before we talked about writing a book, you were encouraging me. You are the only person in the world that I could trust to tell my story and I am so grateful that you believed in me even before I believed in myself. You have shown me a Greenlight to the future.

To Ms. Eunkoo Lee. Thank you for supporting North Korean refugees. Your hard work behind-the-scenes as co-founder of Freedom Speakers International may not always get noticed, but you have made a difference in the lives of many North Korean refugees.

Thank you to Freedom Speakers International. Your assistance to North Korean refugees helps us build our skills and "seize the day" to help us have better lives. I felt so warm when I learned about this great organization. It seemed that North Korean refugees like me weren't alone. I joined when I was looking to improve my English, I started working there part-time, and now I am an author.

Thank you, Mr. James Lee and Mrs. Jane Park (owners of the Haanong Furniture Company). Your support allowed me to focus on writing this book.

Second, I want to thank several people who I haven't met directly or only briefly but who have been supporters and cheerleaders for this book. Thank you, Mr. Paul Grossman. Your support behind-the-scenes helped make this book possible. It was touching to hear how much of an impact reading the manuscript had on you.

Mrs. Eben Appleton became a cheerleader for this book even before she had read it. I am sure that everyone in Gallatin, Tennessee knows who I am. Whenever I sent emails thanking everyone for supporting me, there was always one person I knew who would answer: Mrs. Eben.

Thank you to Mr. Ken Stuart for always remembering details, like my birthday and my son's birthday, and cheering me on whenever possible. Thank you, Mr. Mike

Ashley, for enthusiastically sharing my story with the members of your mother's church. Thank you, Ms. Elizabeth Kim and Sophilia An for becoming cheerleaders of my book and sharing it with your family and friends. Thank you, Ms. Pam Davidson, for being a monthly donor to support the book. Thank you, Mr. Sungbo Shim, for recently becoming an important mentor for me. Thank you, Ms. Suzanne Scholte, Mr. Jason West, and members of the North Korea Freedom Coalition for your support. Thank you, Mr. Mark Bendul, for your support for the book and for being one of my tutors. Thank you, Mr. Arlo Matisz, for your interest in sharing my story in Canada, my freedom country. Thank you to Mr. Donald Kirk for your long-term interest in North Korean refugees, North Korea, and this book. Thank you, Mr. Erick Mertz, for making the book look so beautiful. Thank you, Mr. John Cerasuolo, for supporting FSI and your warm support for this book.

Thank you to members of the FSI-Global High School Union. In particular, thank you Hyowon Gu, Minjae Kim, Toni Ban, Sang Yoon Lee, Hyungmin Song, Timothy Han, Wonhyuk Choi, and Dongyeon Kim. You ordered so many copies of this book in advance so you could donate them to libraries in the USA. When I was in North Korea, I didn't study beyond one year of elementary school. Now, thanks to you, my book will be in libraries in all 50 US states. My heart leaped when I saw the video made by so many of you informing people about this book. Thank you, Teri Shim, for making a special animation about me and Mom. Whenever I feel a little down, I watch that video and I feel so warm.

Thank you FSI staff, interns, and volunteers for

helping make this book possible. Thank you, Ms. Brooke Chong, for your assistance with the publication process. Thank you, Ms. Ingrid Knudsen, for publicizing this book on FSI's SNS. Thank you, Ms. Dahye Kang, for your graphic designs and videos publicizing *Greenlight to Freedom*. Thank you, Hope French, for recording my speeches so I could use proper pronunciation. Thank you, Ms. Irene Yoon, chief editor of this book. You have a sharp eye and you caught so many typos and corrected so much of my Konglish. Thank you, Mr. Michael Donmoyer, assistant editor of this book. I am sure that you and Ms. Irene had a very tough time editing this book.

Third, I want to thank people who didn't help with the book but have been important in my life in some way. Thank you to my aunts in North Korea. To Aunt Yeonhui: it wasn't always smooth and I had mixed feelings about our relationship in the past. Writing this book made me realize how lucky I was that you let me live with you for several years. Without you, I could have been homeless or even starved to death. Thank you to Aunt Seonhui for always encouraging me and believing that Mom would find me one day. You told me not to forget about you if I ever reunited with Mom, and I haven't forgotten about you. I hope we can meet in freedom one day.

Thank you to Grandma Bae and Uncle Gicheol. You were so loving and sweet to me when I was young and I will never forget you. I really hope I can see you again at least once in this life. I hope I can scream your name and have you answer at least once, Grandma. And Uncle Gicheol, I am much stronger now, and I hope you too are much stronger so I can throw a pillow at you again. My son is playful, too, so he might throw pillows at you too.

To my cousins who encouraged me when I was in

North Korea: thank you for believing that Mom would come to me one day. I am sorry that we can't be together now. You asked me to rescue you if I ever made it to freedom. Mom misses you now and wishes we could all be together again.

To the North Koreans who went to the mountain with me to collect wood: thank you. I didn't feel like I was alone when you went with me. Chunhui, in particular, thank you for being with me during those difficult times. Because you are deaf, we used body language and sign language to communicate. We were so close and I hope you are doing well and that we can see each other again one day.

To the counselors at the counseling center: thank you for helping me get over my trauma and finding myself. I was hostile in the beginning when I wasn't ready to talk about my problems. You helped me open up, so I could confront my trauma and mixed feelings about my childhood. I changed in many ways because of counseling. I am thankful you were so patient with me.

There are three very good friends who prefer to remain anonymous but who are always there for me. One of my good friends always encourages me with beautiful words. I rarely heard praise when I was in North Korea. "You are amazing" is something I can hear from her every time we talk. Even if I am just planning to do something, she will praise me for that. It is easy to find people ready to criticize you, so it is comforting to have someone always on your side. Then I think to myself, "She believes in me." Her praise raises my expectations for myself. She believes in me, so that means that I really need to do it! Another friend always wants to help me. She's not rich, but she shares with me everything that she can. She is someone, at my most vulnerable moments, that I know I can always rely on.

One of my best friends, also from North Korea, listens to everything I say. I can trust her with my most personal things. If I have a problem, then she is angrier about it than I am. If I say that someone has hurt me or even just makes me feel bad, then she says, "Okay, let's go get him." Then we laugh and talk about how lucky we are to have escaped from North Korea.

To young children and even adults around the world waiting for your parents, you may feel unloved, unwanted, and may blame your parents or yourselves for the separation. I hope you can find peace and be reunited with your loved ones as I have. For parents separated from your children, I feel so sorry that many of you can only embrace them in your hearts. You may feel guilty about leaving your children behind. If you aren't sure if your children will accept you, I hope you will do as my mother did and try to be together again.

Finally, thank you to everyone who has supported this book. Every day, I feel thankful to be alive and so happy with the nice people in my life. Every moment is important. I enjoy breathing in the air, seeing the world around me, and being able to move and enjoy my life. I am grateful to be alive and so thankful that you have become part of my life. I know that I am not alone in this world.

ABOUT THE AUTHORS

SONGMI HAN was born in Geumya-gun, Bongsan-ri in the center of North Korea about 240 kilometers (150 miles) from the capital of Pyongyang. She escaped from North Korea in 2011, and settled in South Korea later that year. She is now a college student studying social welfare at a university outside of Seoul, a keynote speaker and special assistant at Freedom Speakers International, and is happy to be living in freedom.

CASEY LARTIGUE JR. is the co-founder and co-president of Freedom Speakers International in Seoul, Korea. He is co-editor of the book *Educational Freedom in Urban America: Brown v. Board after Half a Century.* He is the 2017 winner of the Special Contribution Award presented by the Hansarang Rural Cultural Foundation, the winner of two awards by Challenge Korea (2018's Global Award and 2019's "Challenge Maker" Award), and in 2021 he was awarded a special Letter of Commendation by the Korea Hana Foundation. He has a bachelor's degree from the Harvard University Extension School and a master's degree from the Harvard Graduate School of Education.

Made in the USA
Las Vegas, NV
01 December 2023

81938826R00174